How To Draw
CUTE ANIMALS

This Book Belongs To:
_____

Grid Copy Drawing Method & Step-By-Step Drawing for Kids

Welcome To
"HOW TO DRAW CUTE ANIMALS"

There is no preparation needed to get going, just take a good pencil and start drawing. Don't forget to have an eraser ready as correcting errors is all part of the fun!

Start your drawings using light pencil strokes, these can always be darkened later with something more permanent. Remain focused on the part you are drawing. It is not a race, so go at a relaxed speed. Draw an outline sketch first, then you can go over it with darker strokes and detail.

The age-old adage of "practice-makes-perfect" applies to drawing too. So, keep drawing, lots!

HOW TO USE THIS BOOK

PART 1 : GRID COPY DRAWING METHOD

Start drawing in box A1 and work along the rows and down the columns, focusing only on the one box you are currently working on.

Draw precisely what is in that small box, nothing else. When you've finished one box, move on to the next.

Try the example below, drawing the image in this 42-box grid. Start at box A1 and draw your way to box F7.

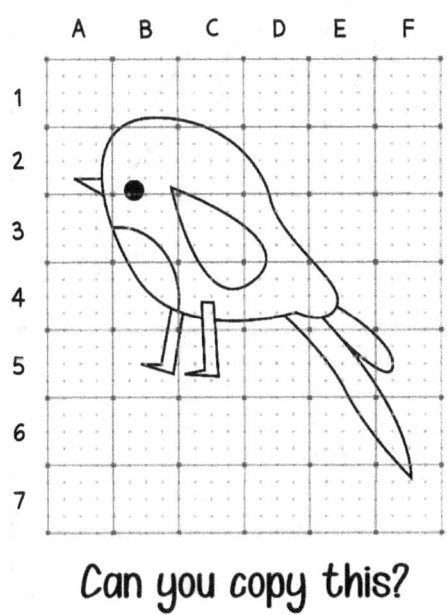

Can you copy this?

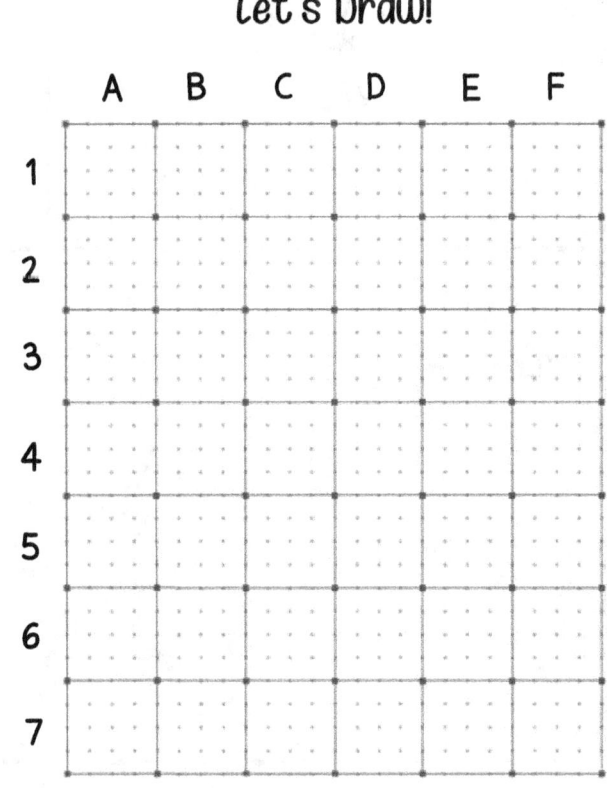

Let's Draw!

PART 2 : STEP-BY-STEP DRAWING

Try the example below, follow the 4 steps to learn how to draw cute animals!

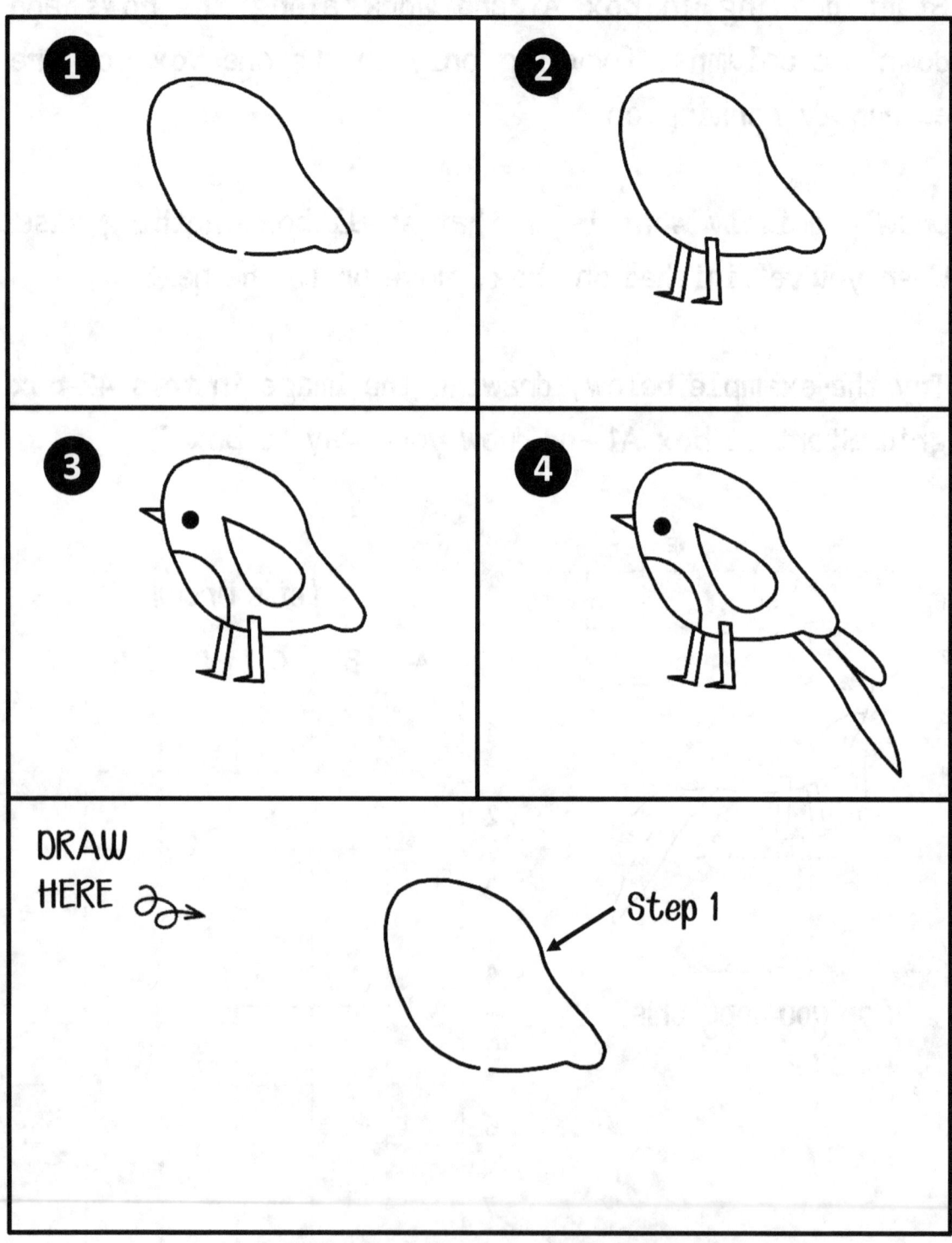

PART 3 : PRACTICE

Use this page to practice your drawing.

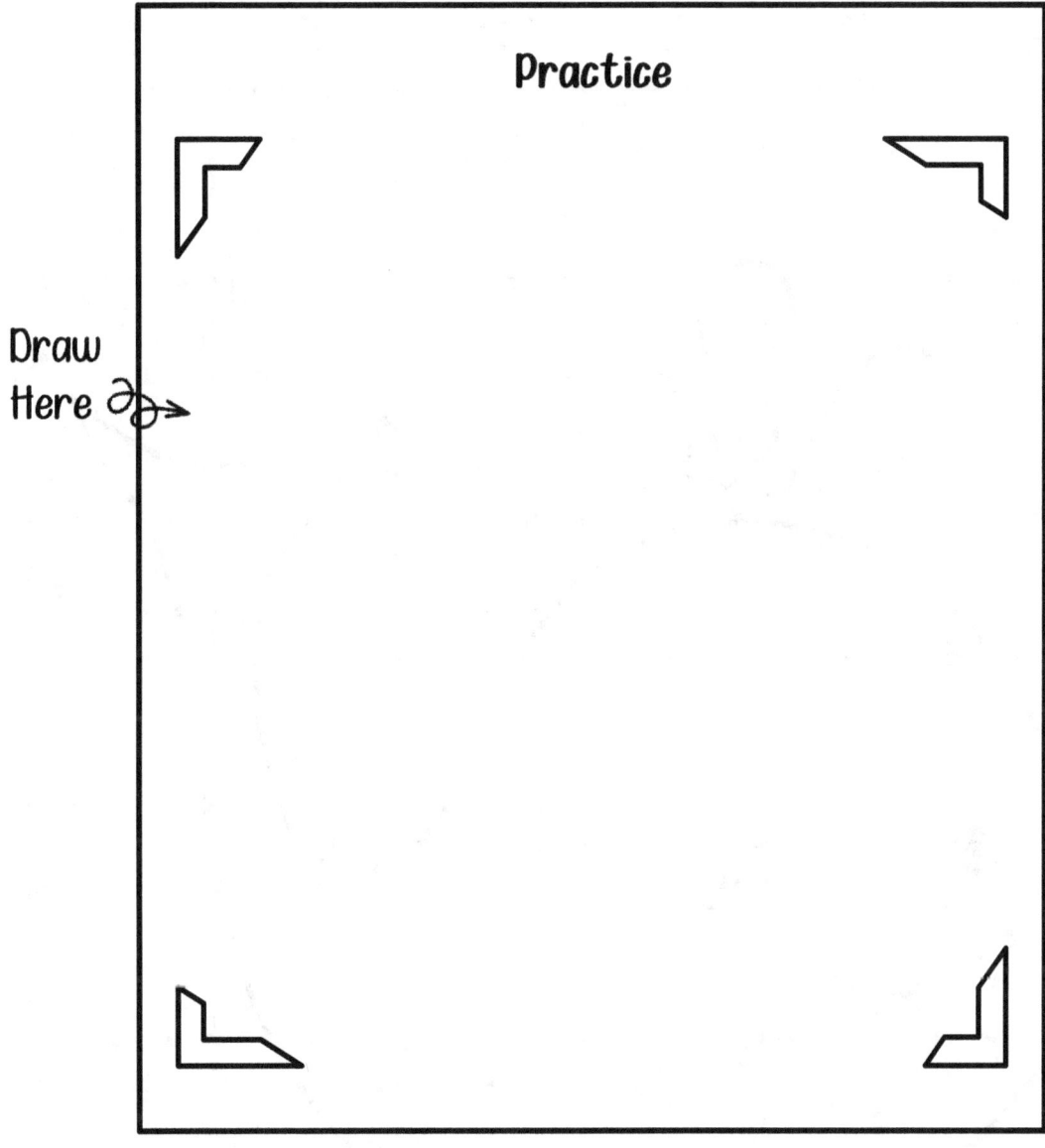

When done, personalize it with your own details and colors. Then step back and admire your excellent work of art! Are you ready? Let's go!

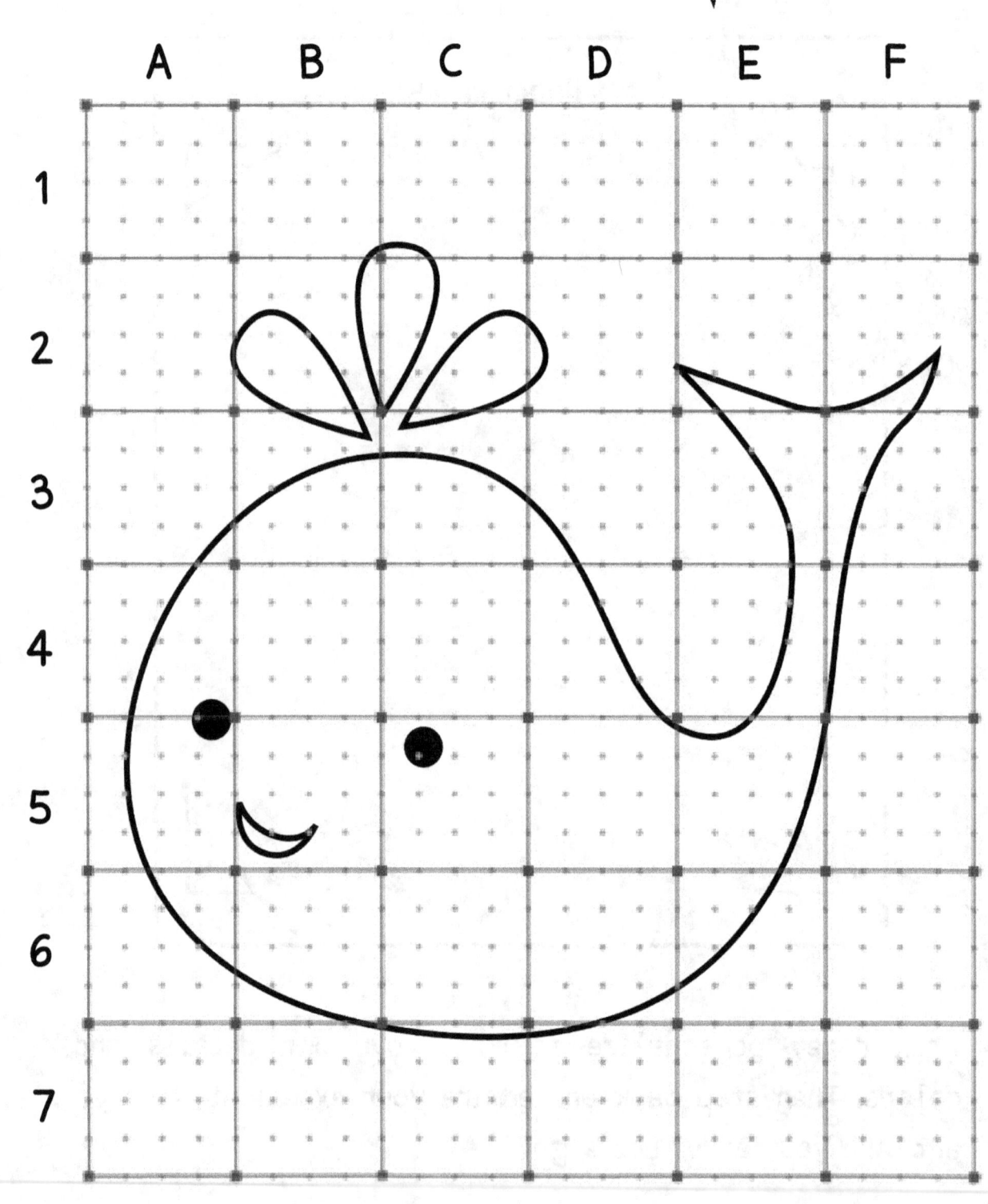

Let's Draw!

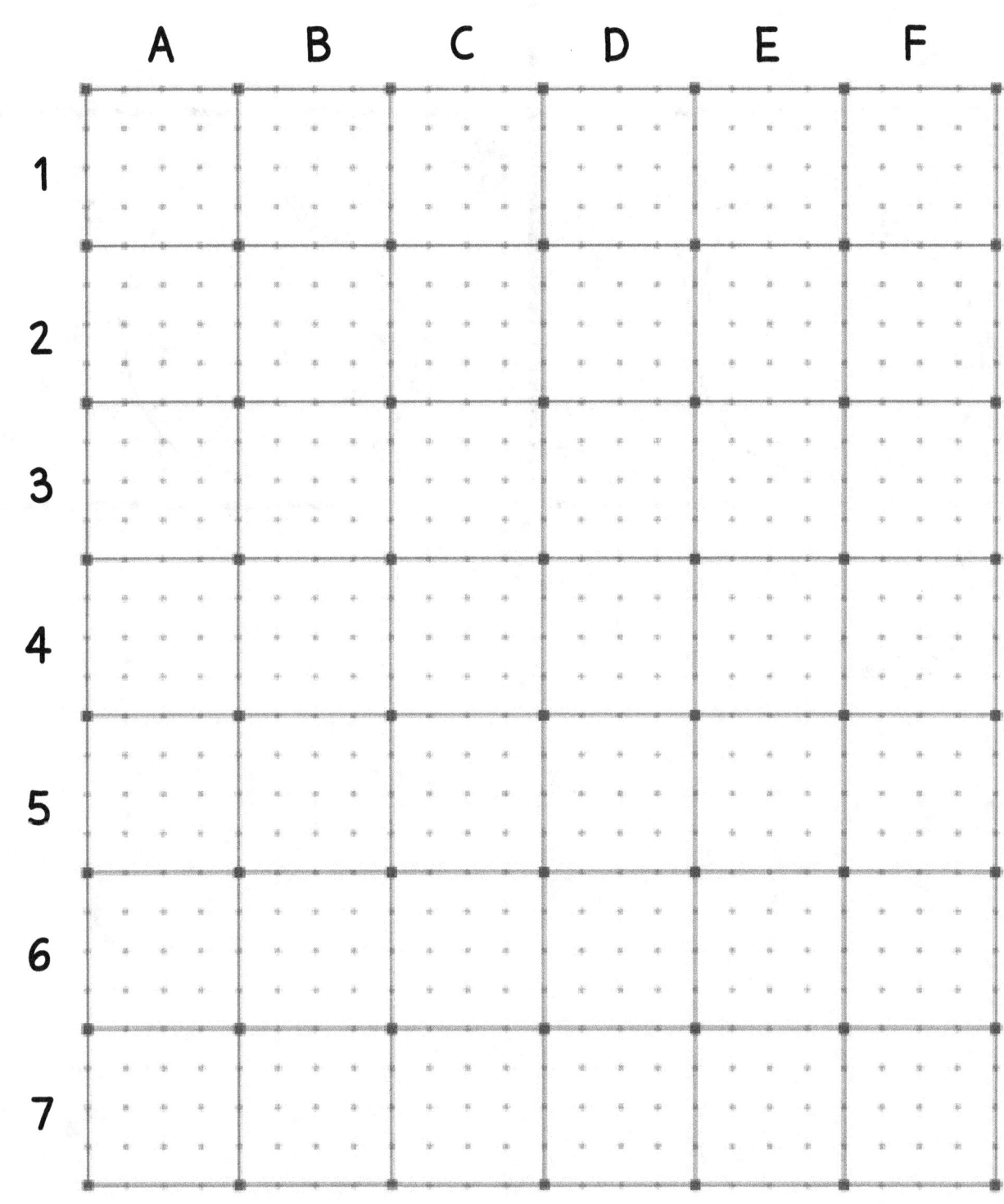

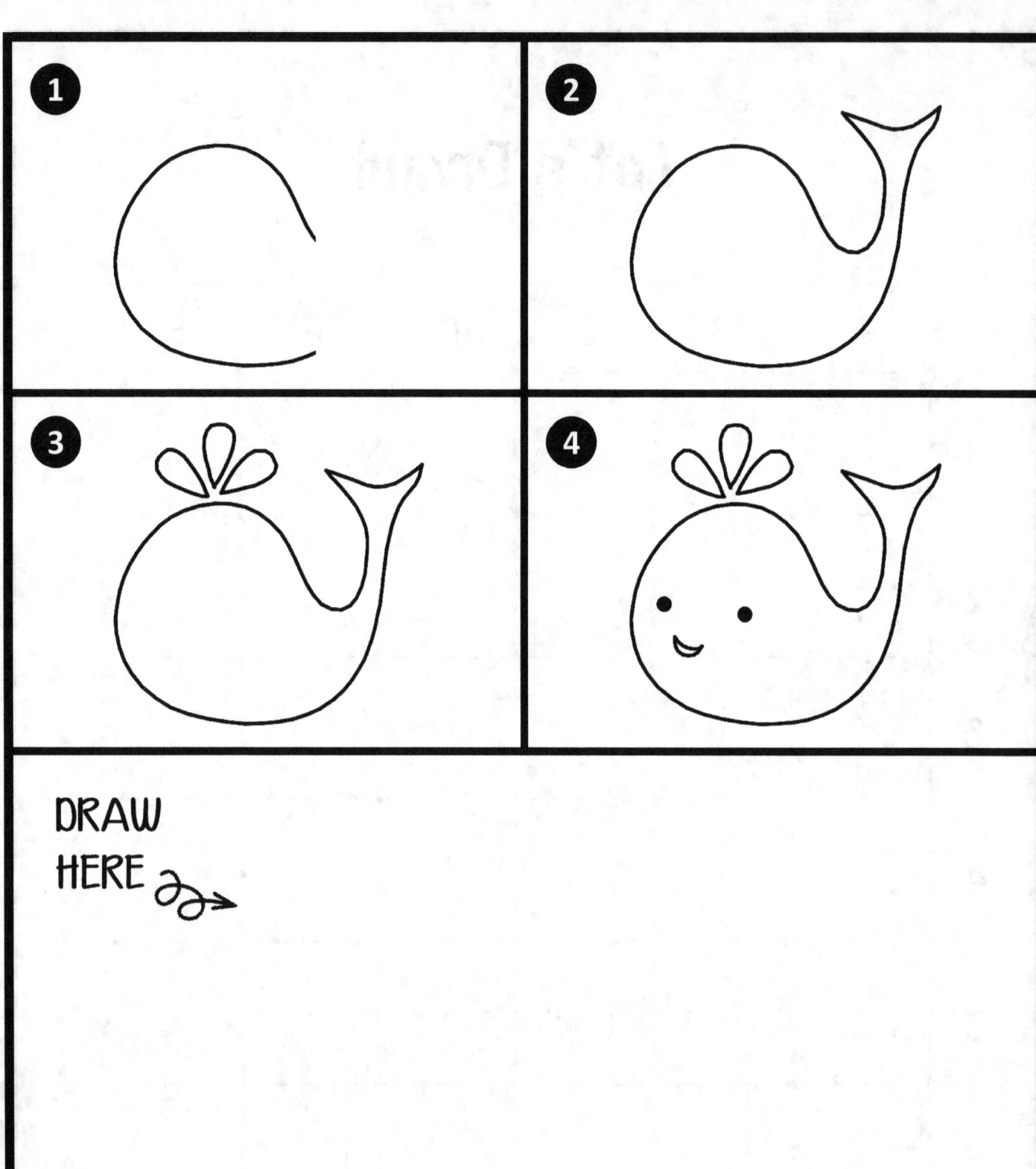

DRAW HERE

Practice

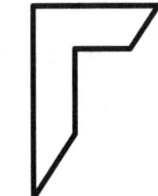
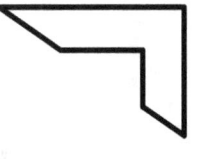
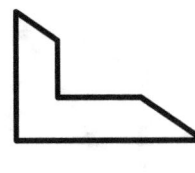
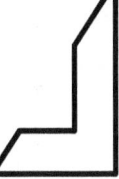

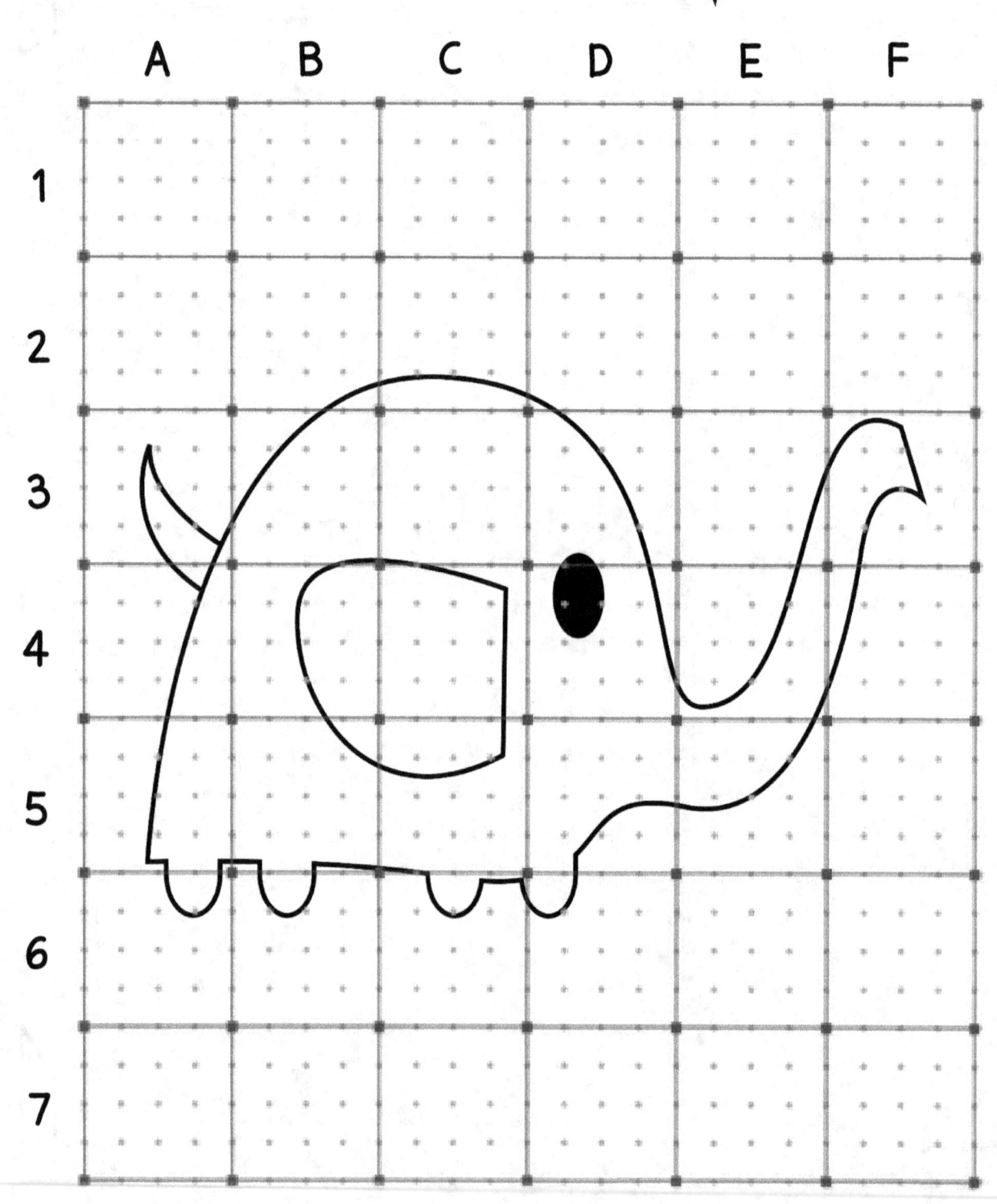

Let's Draw!

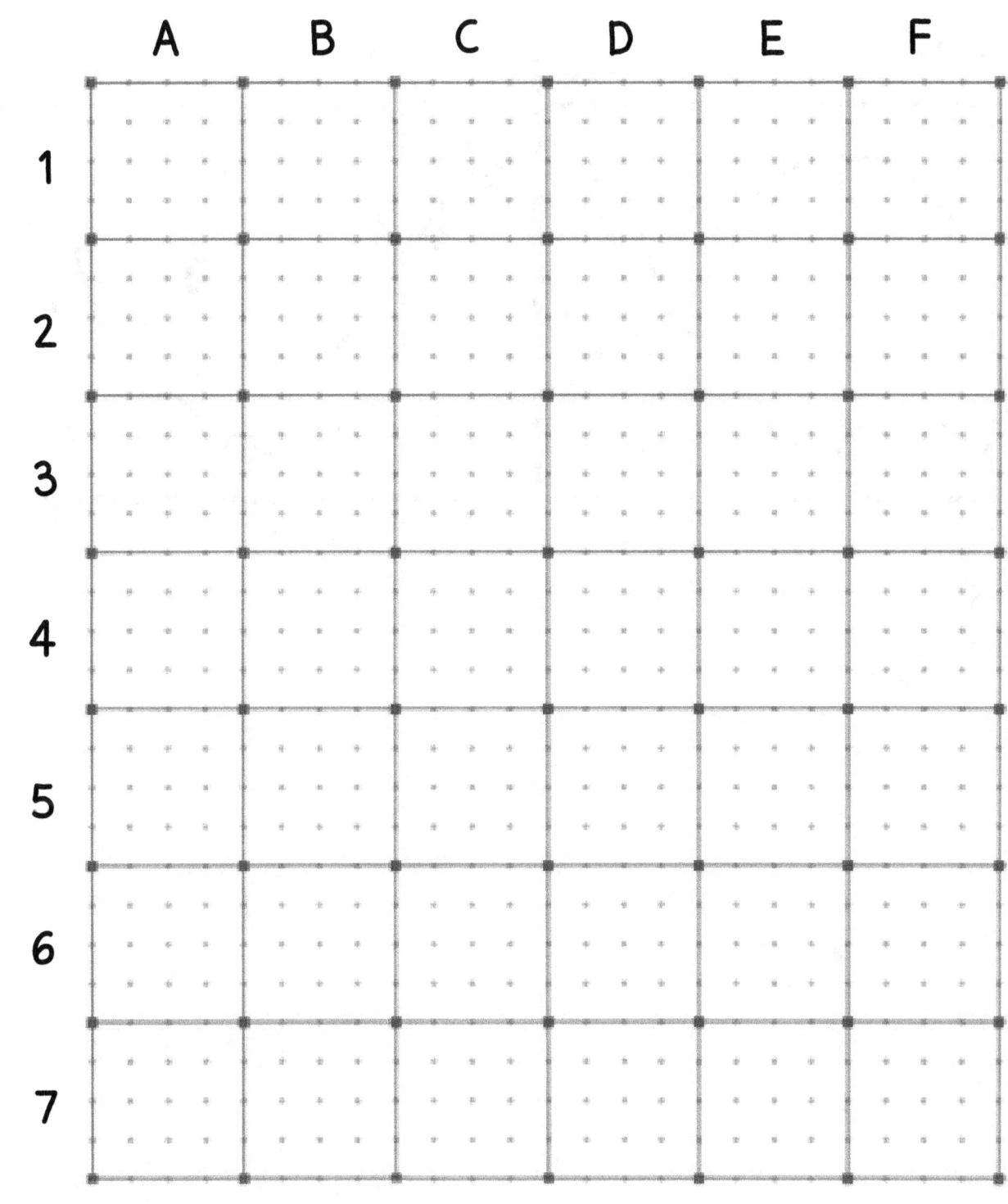

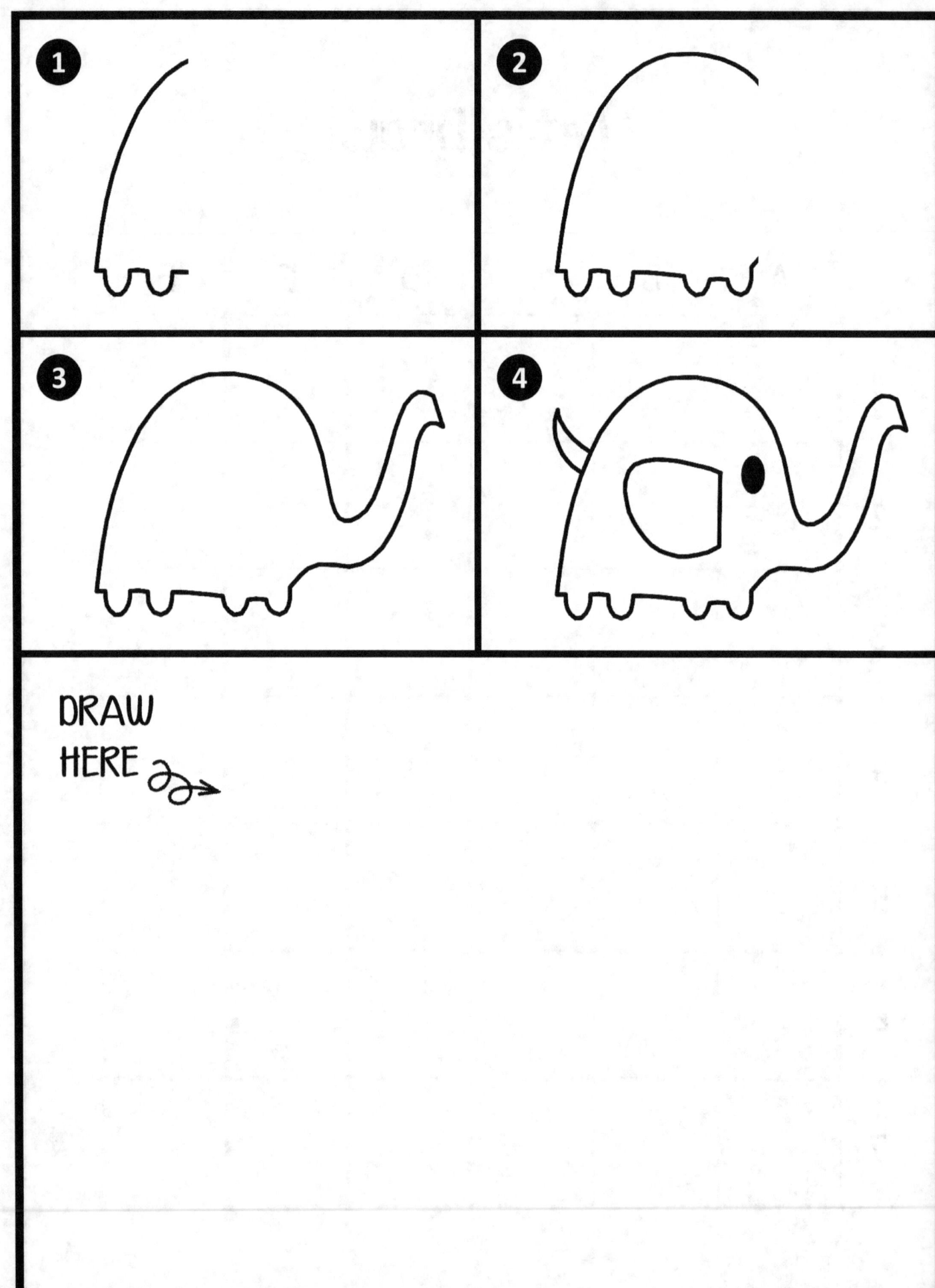

Practice

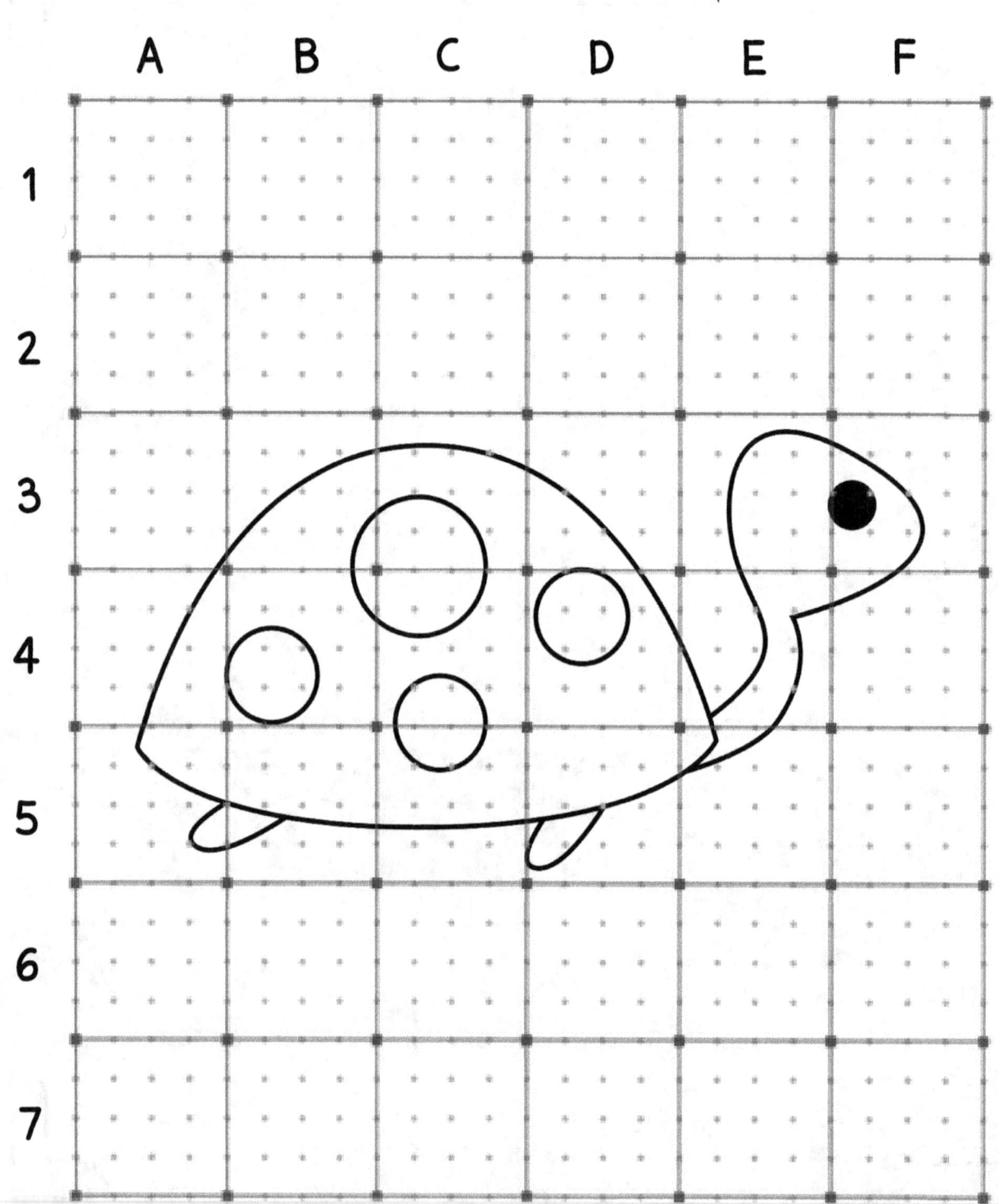

Let's Draw!

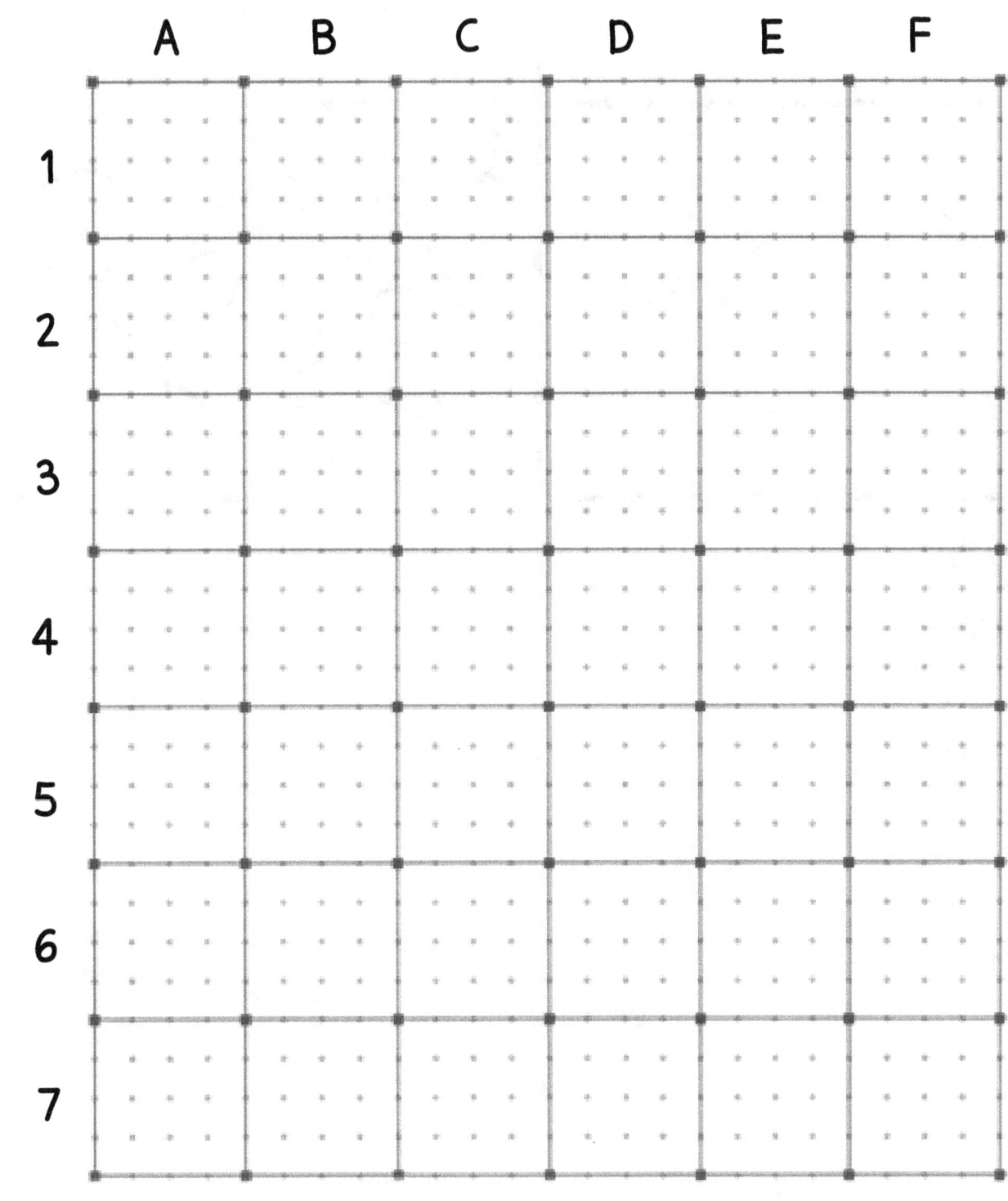

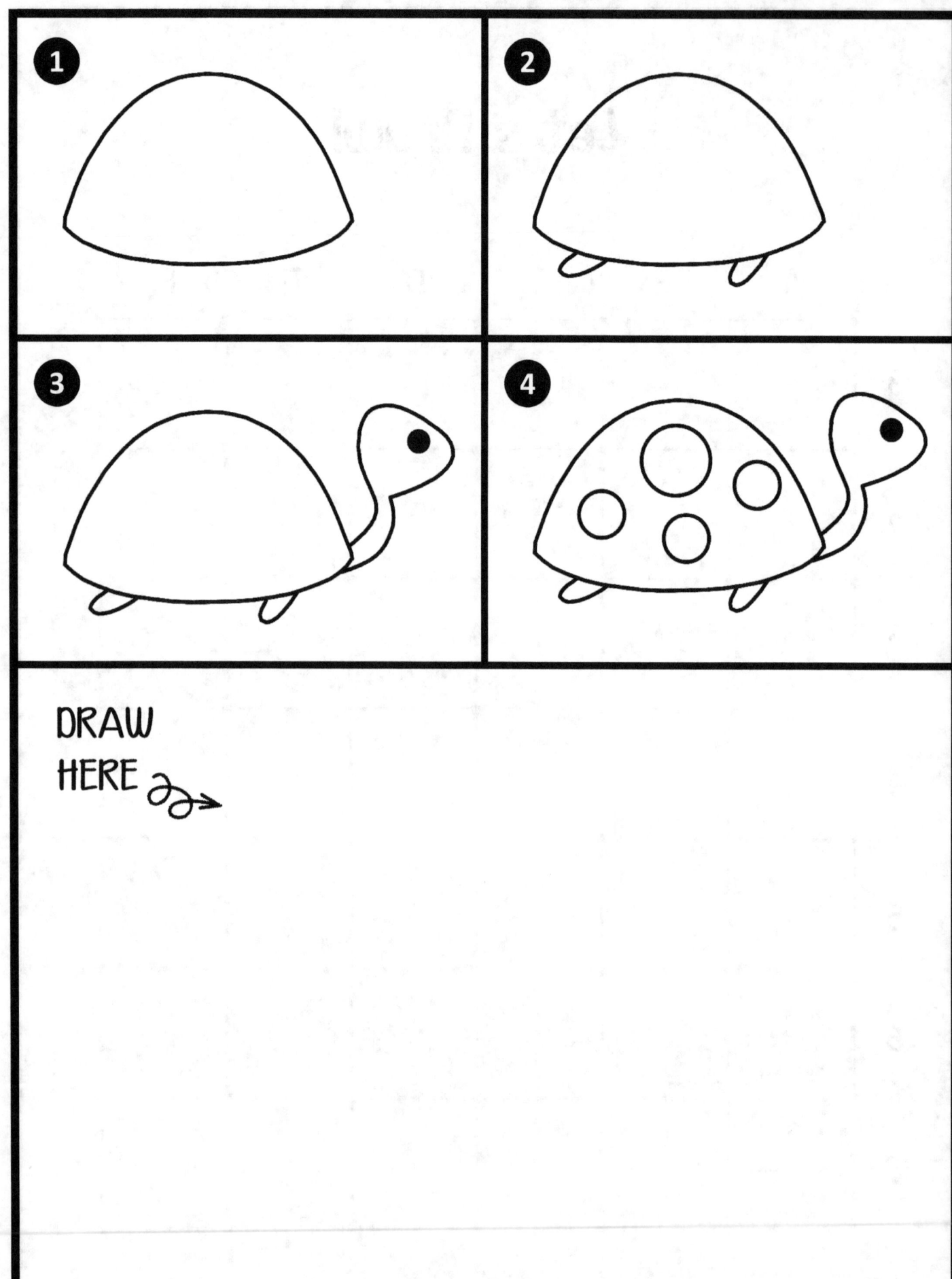

Practice

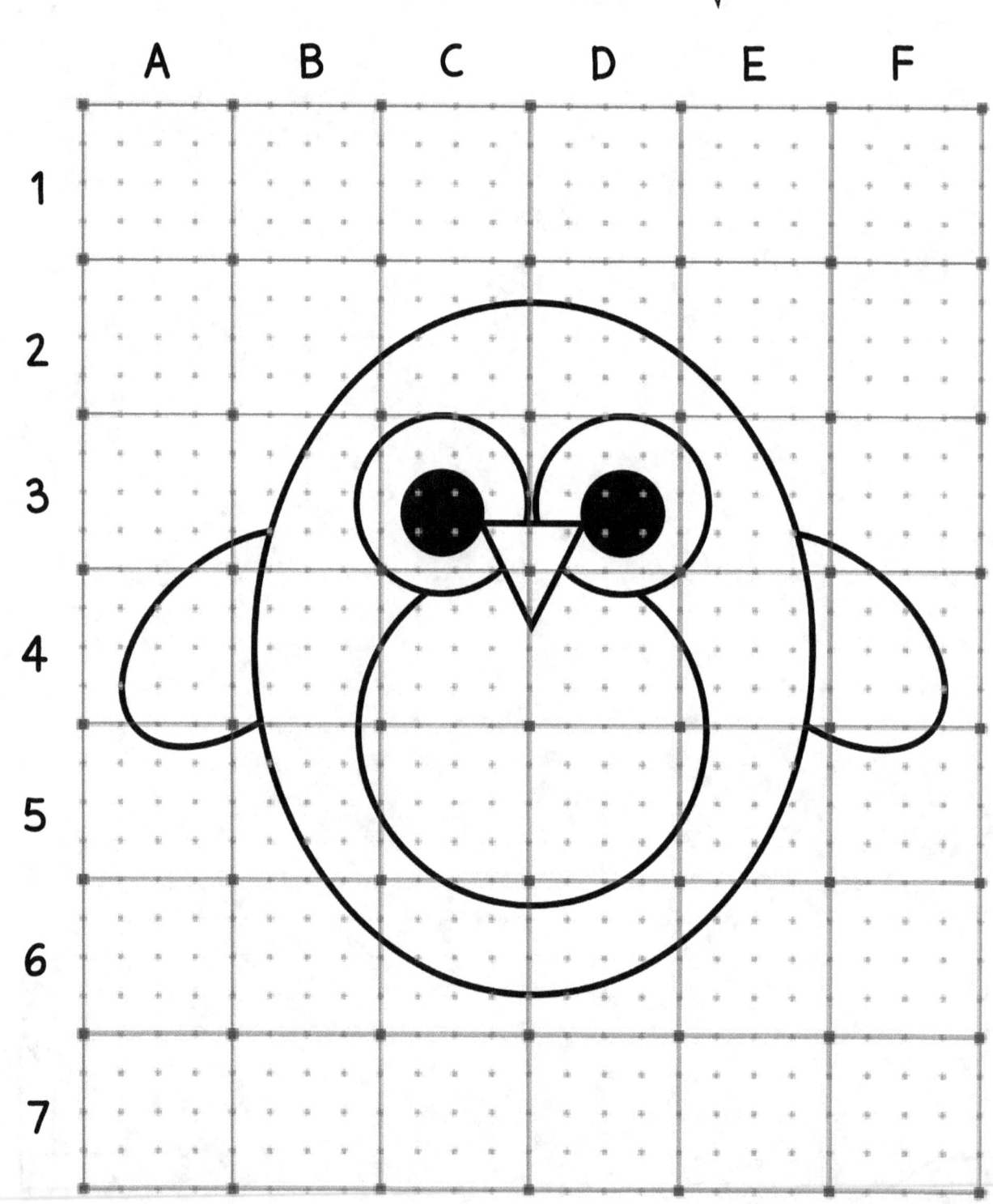

Let's Draw!

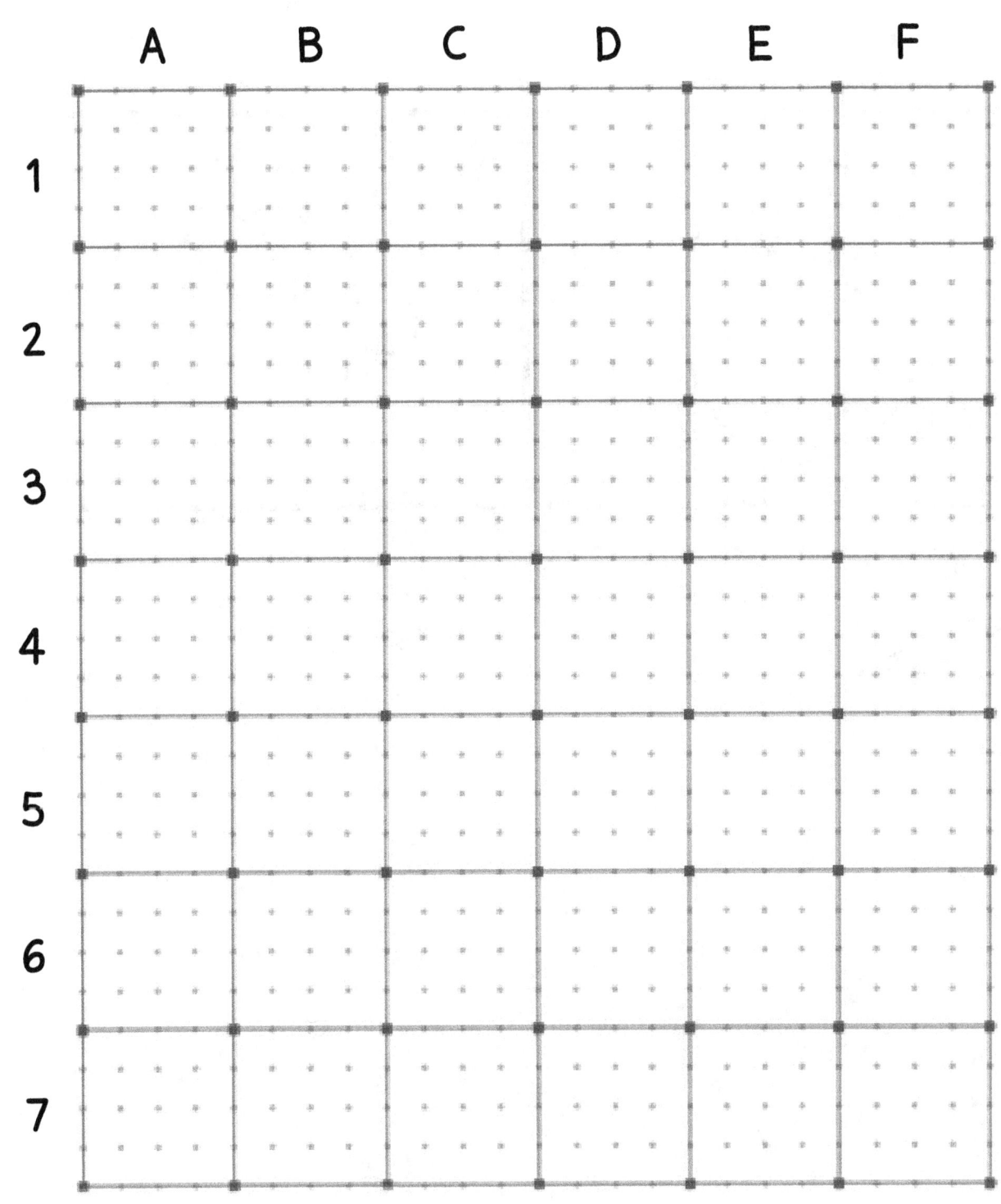

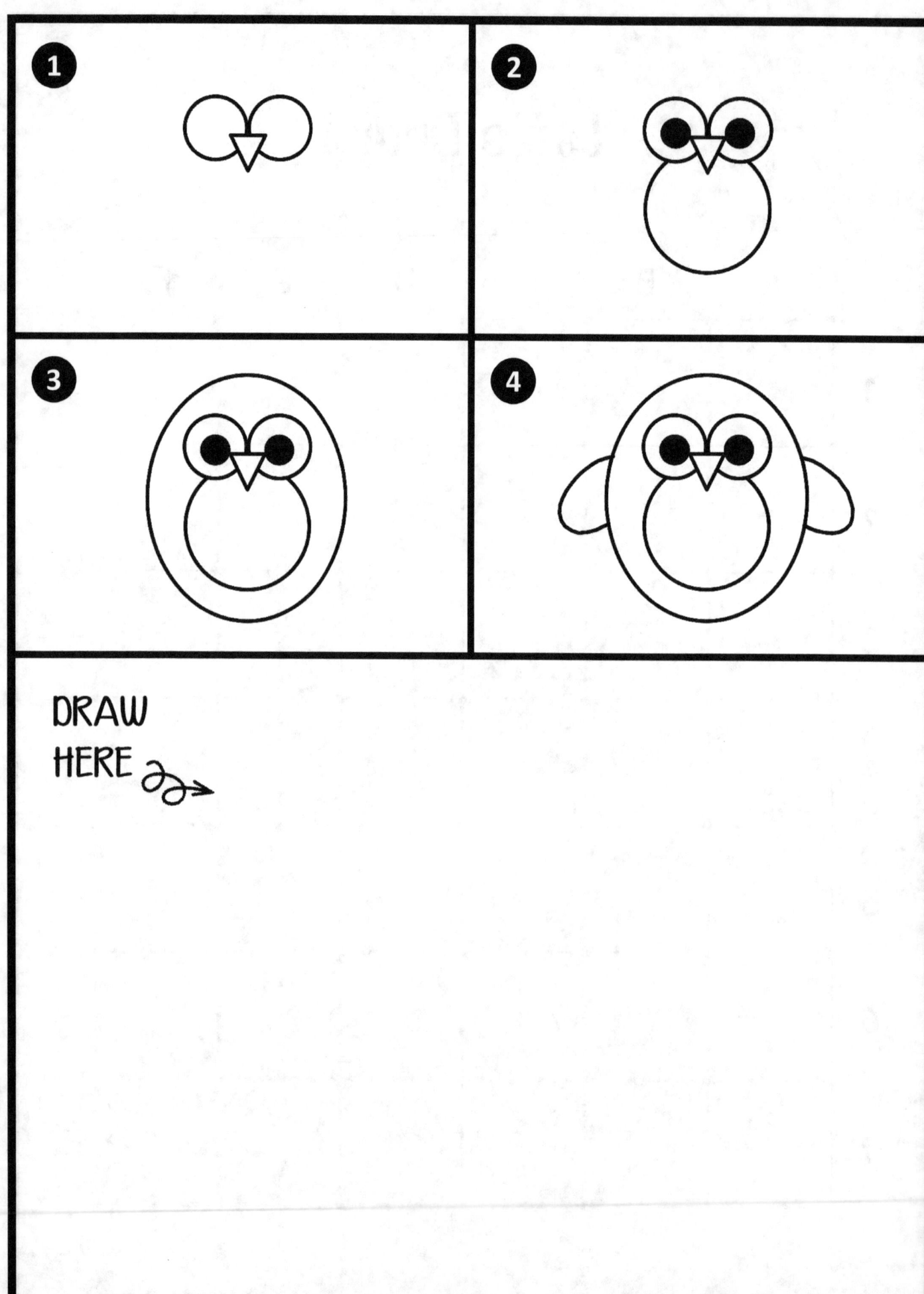

Practice

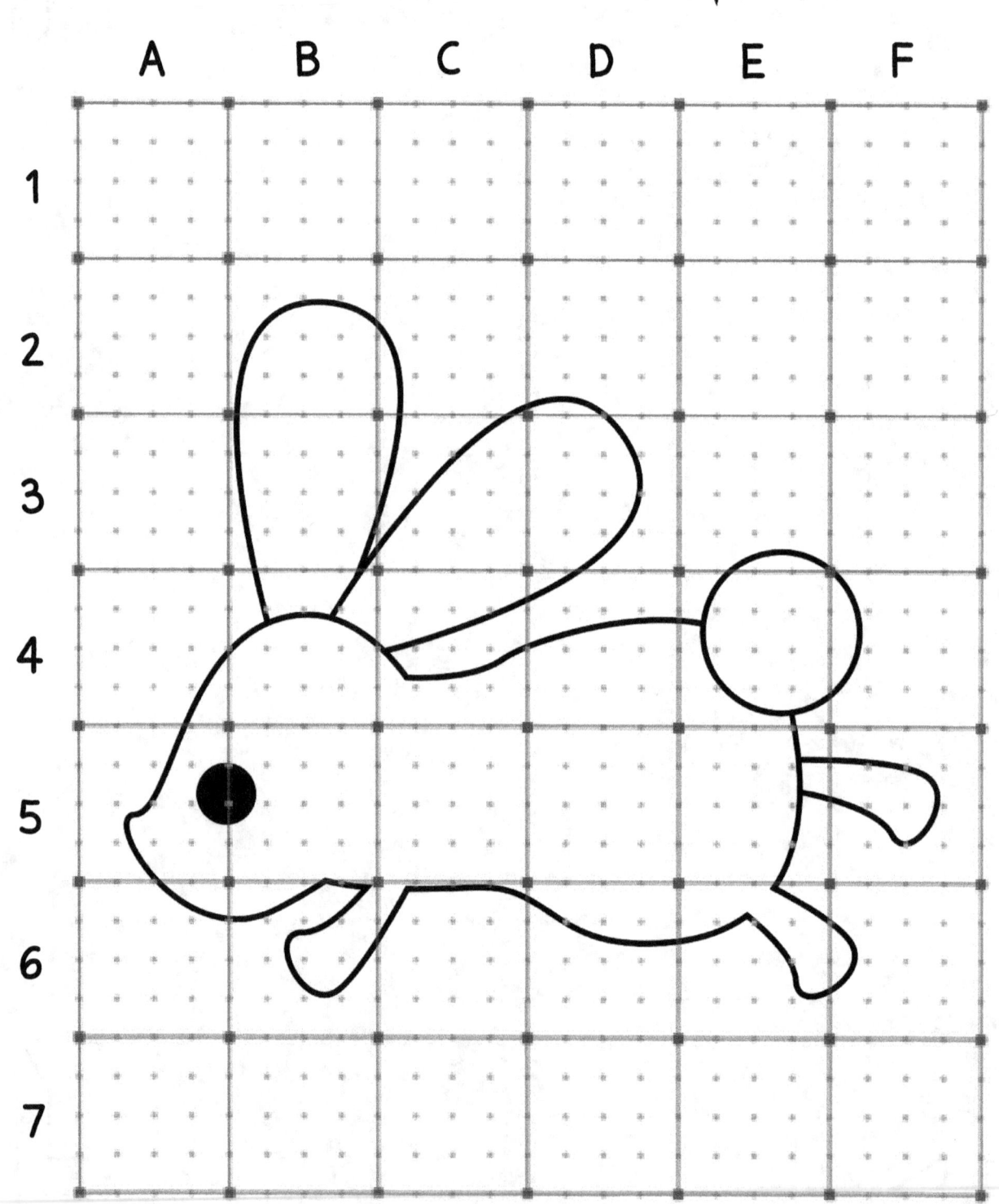

Let's Draw!

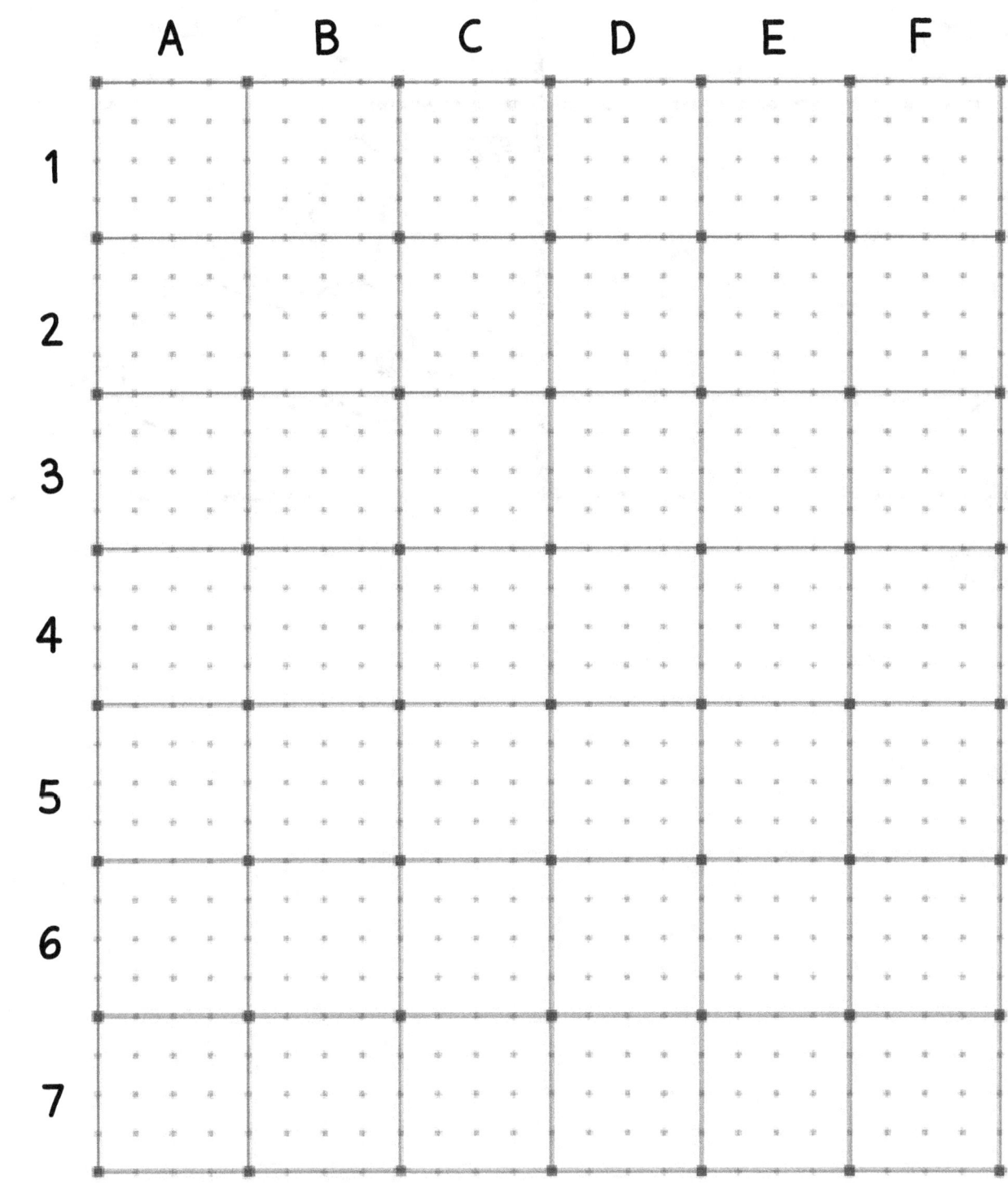

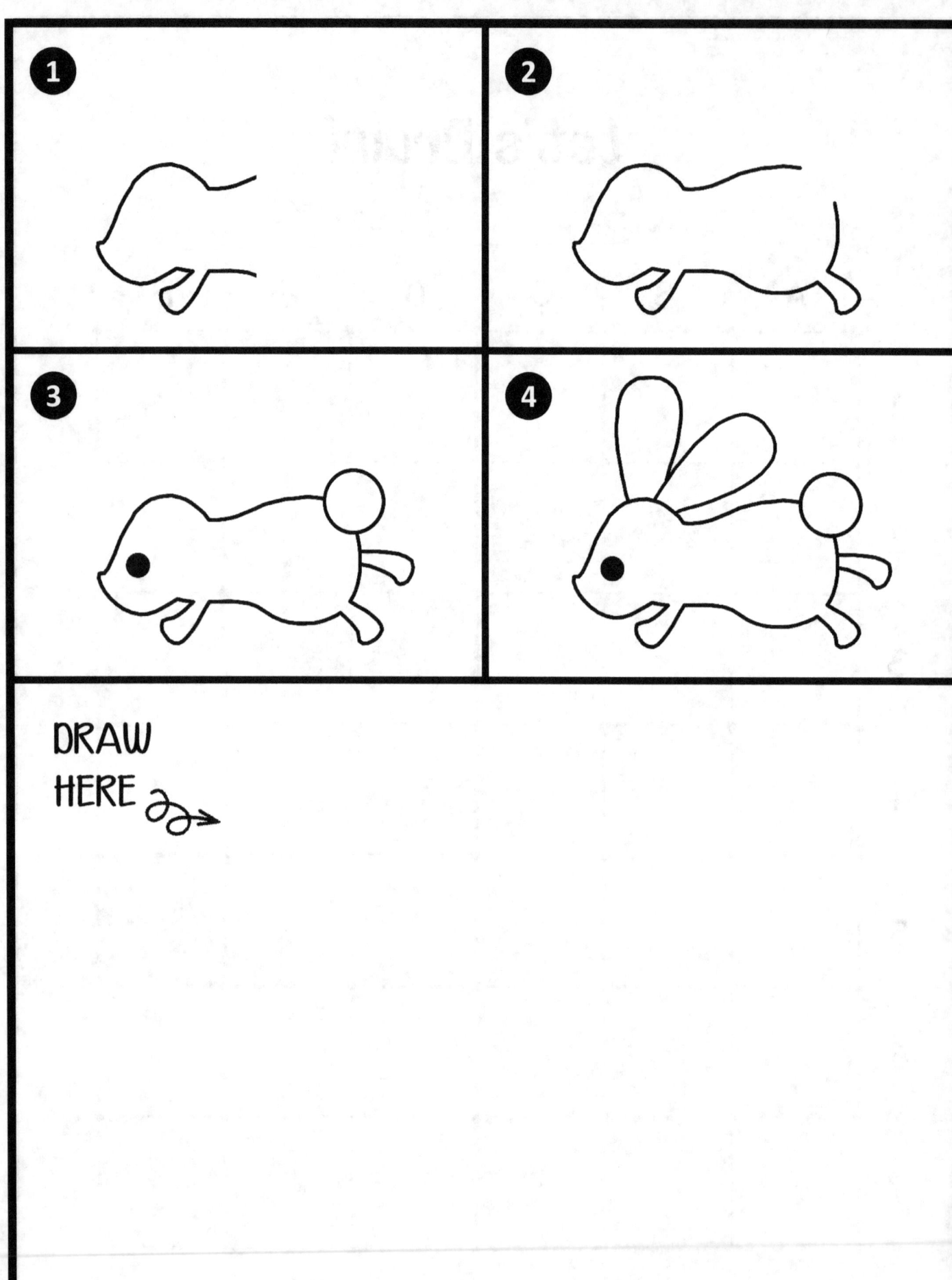

Practice

FROG

A B C D E F

Let's Draw!

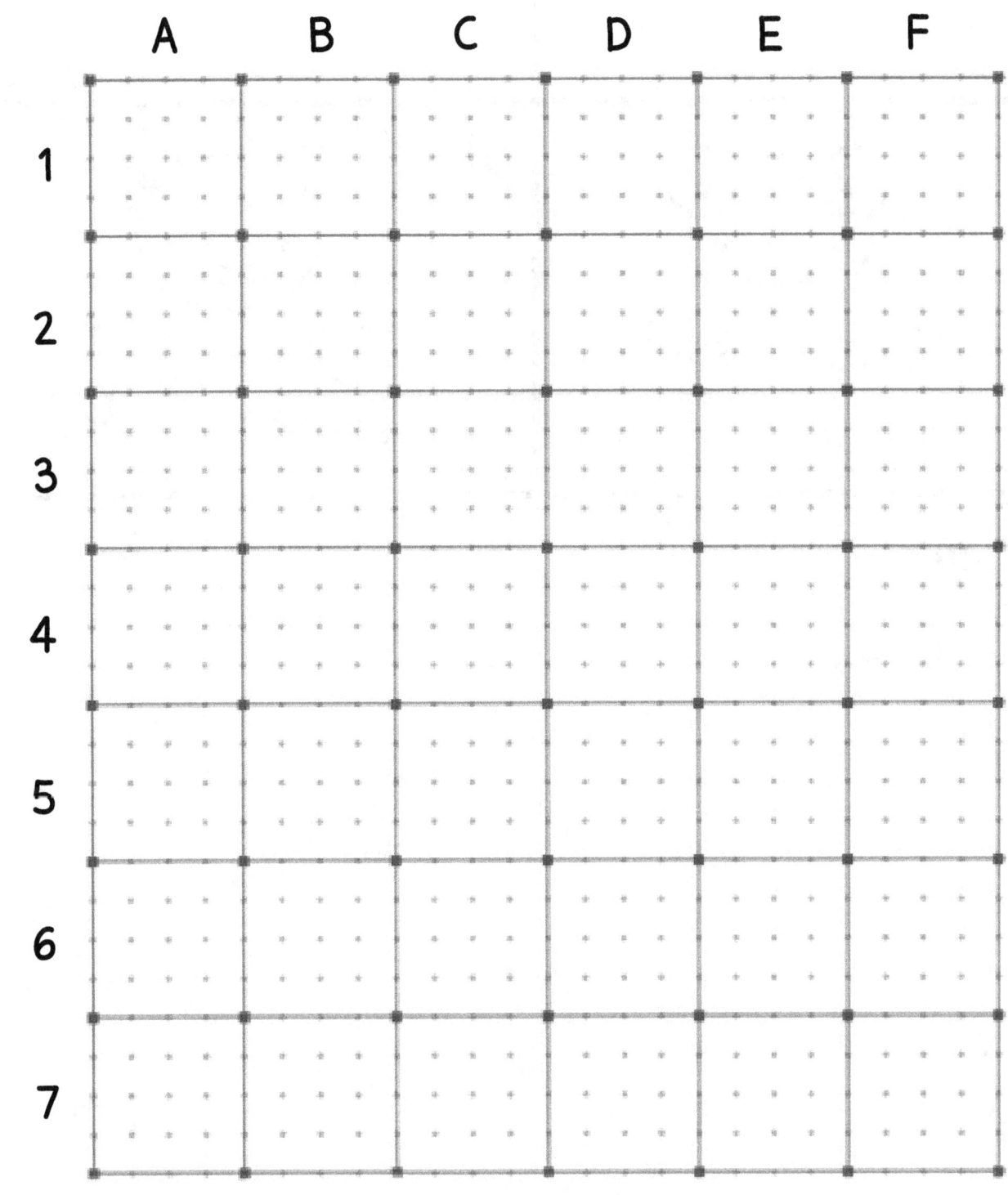

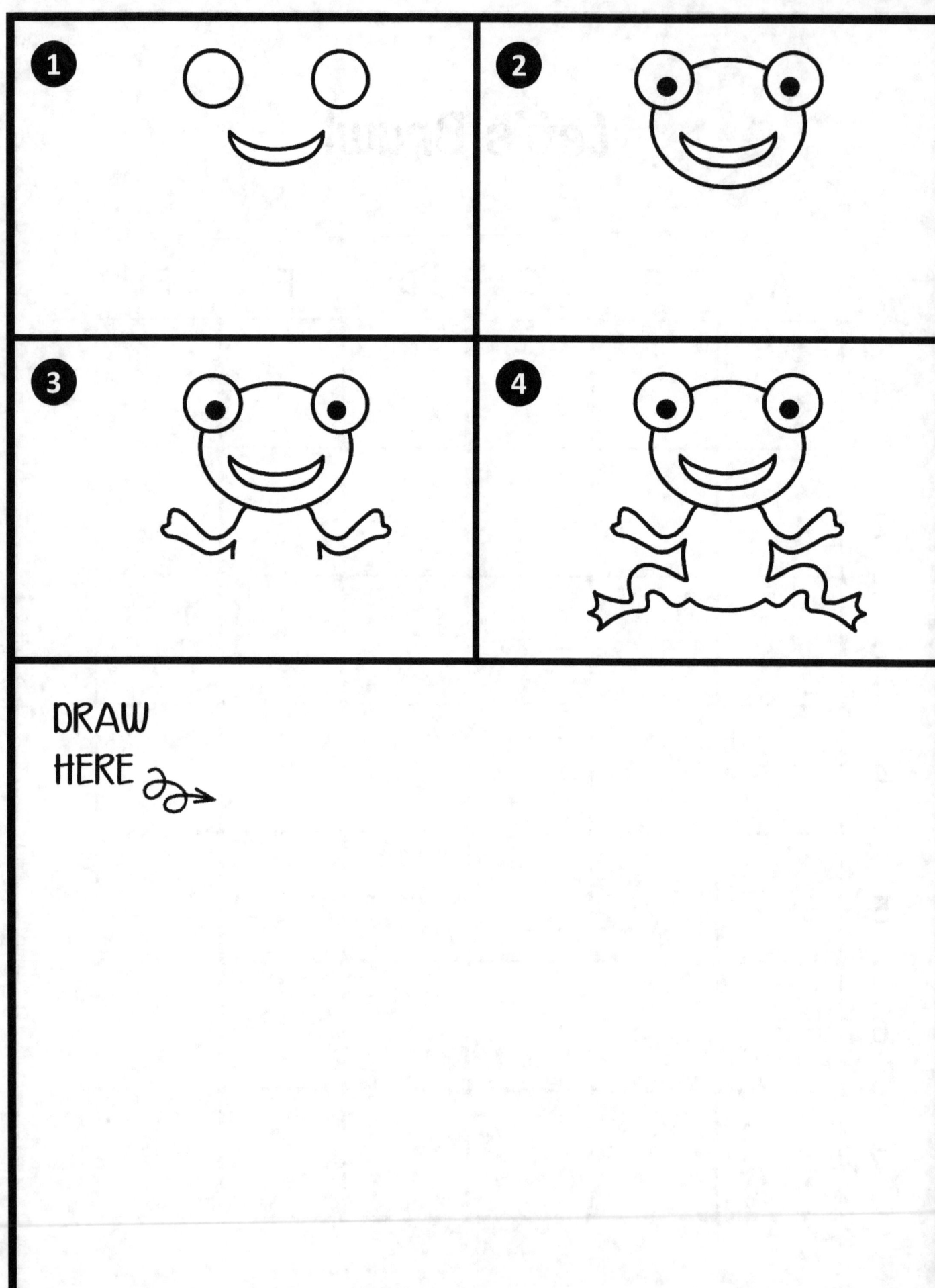

Practice

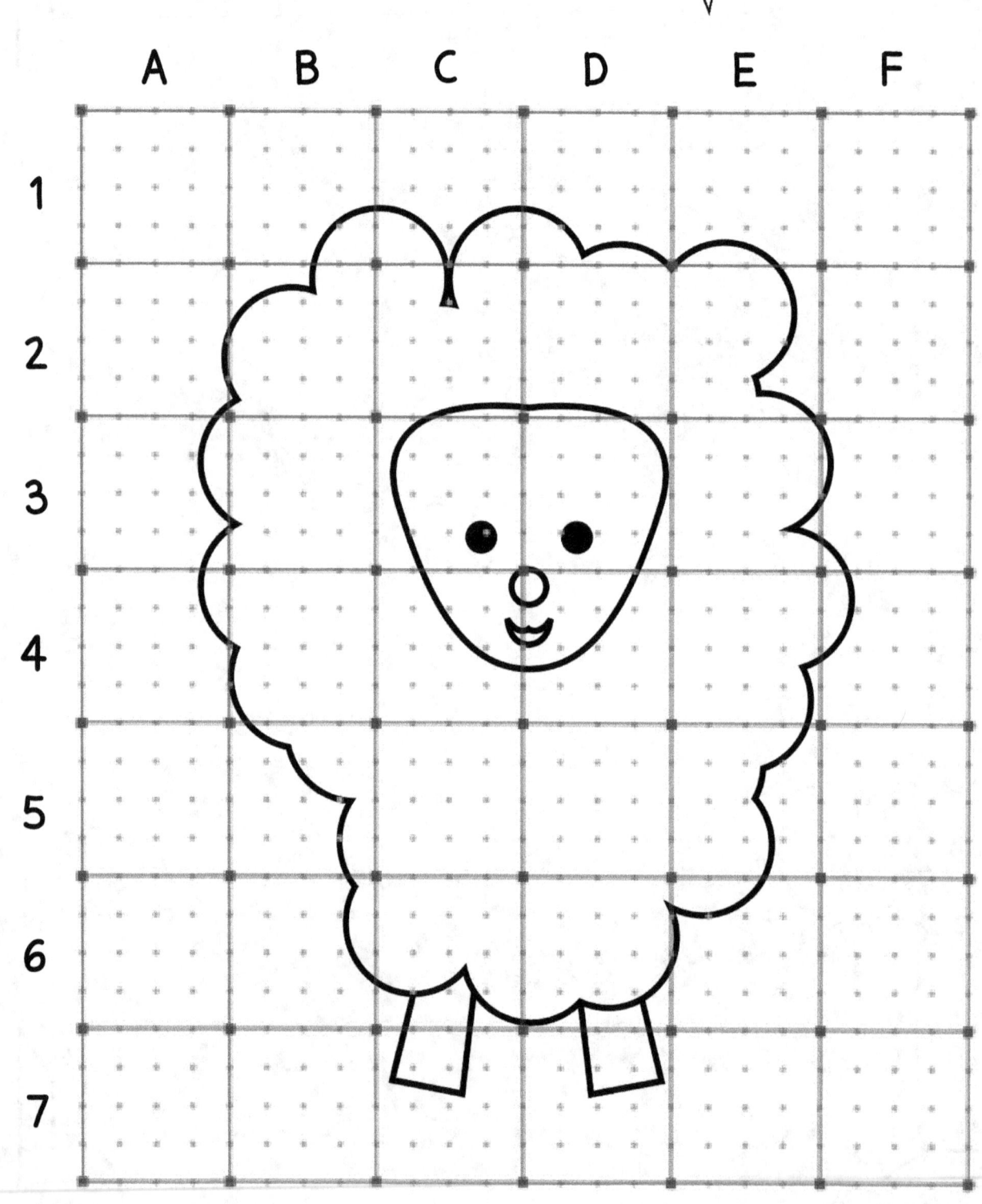

Let's Draw!

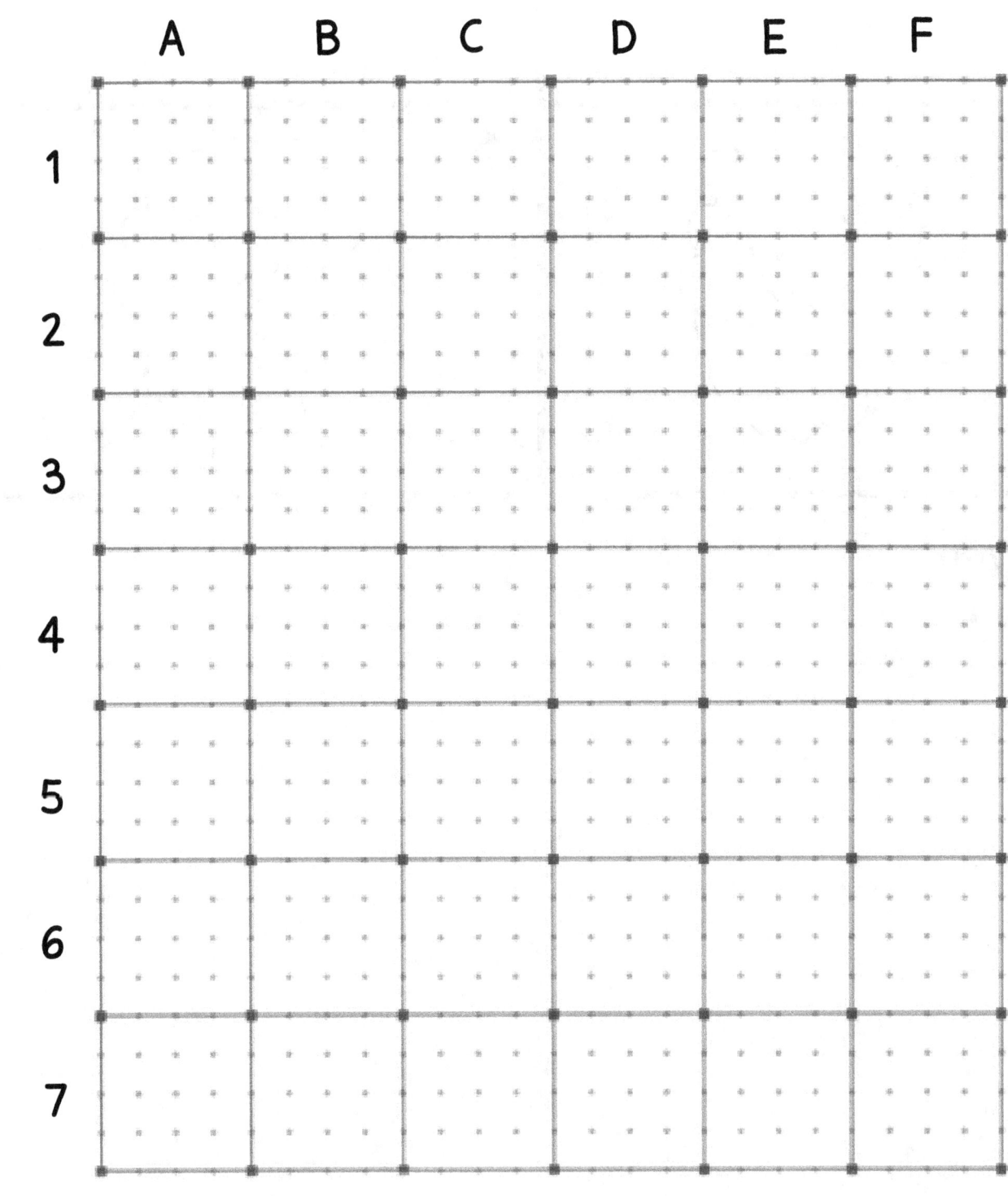

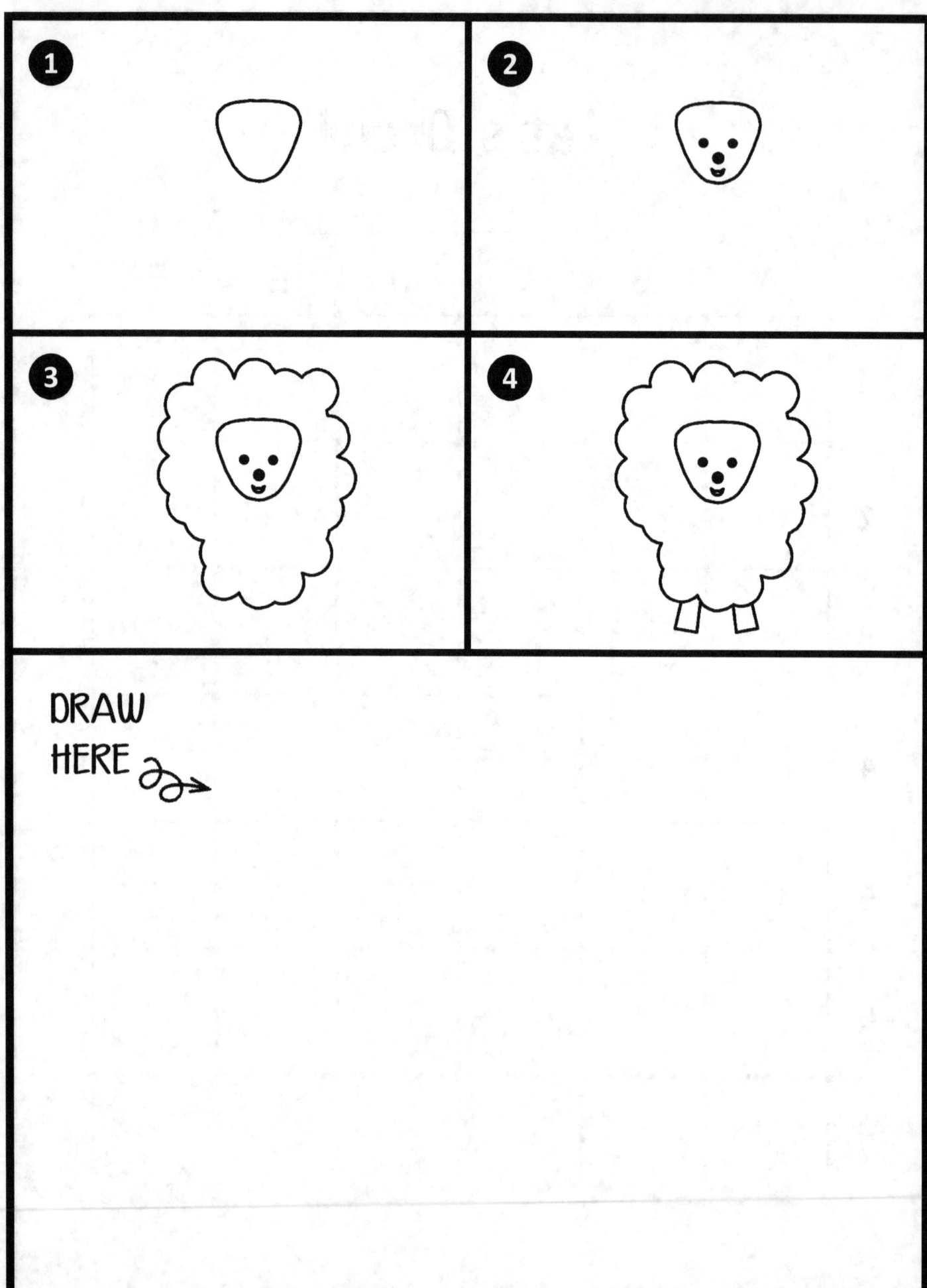

Practice

COW

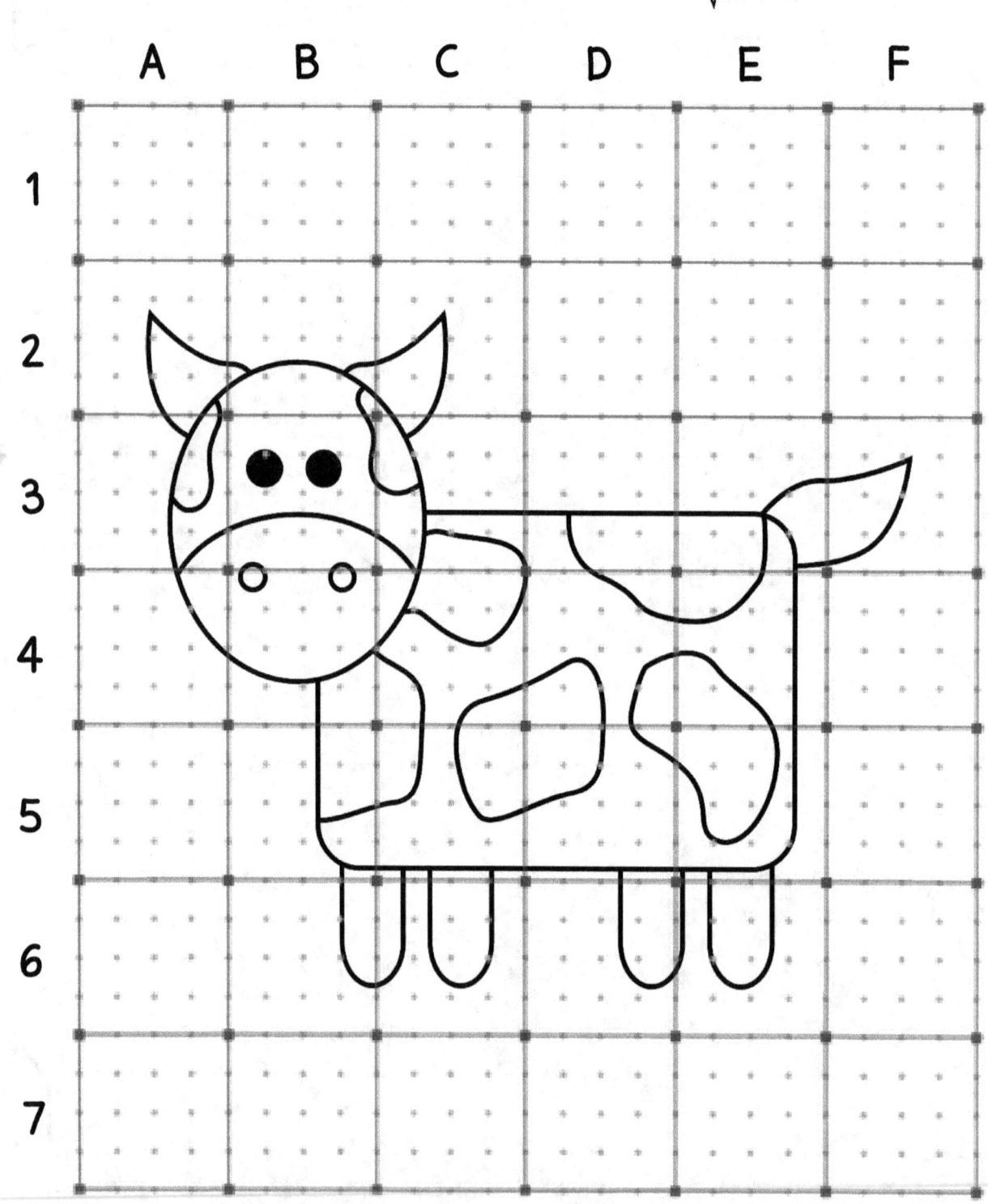

Let's Draw!

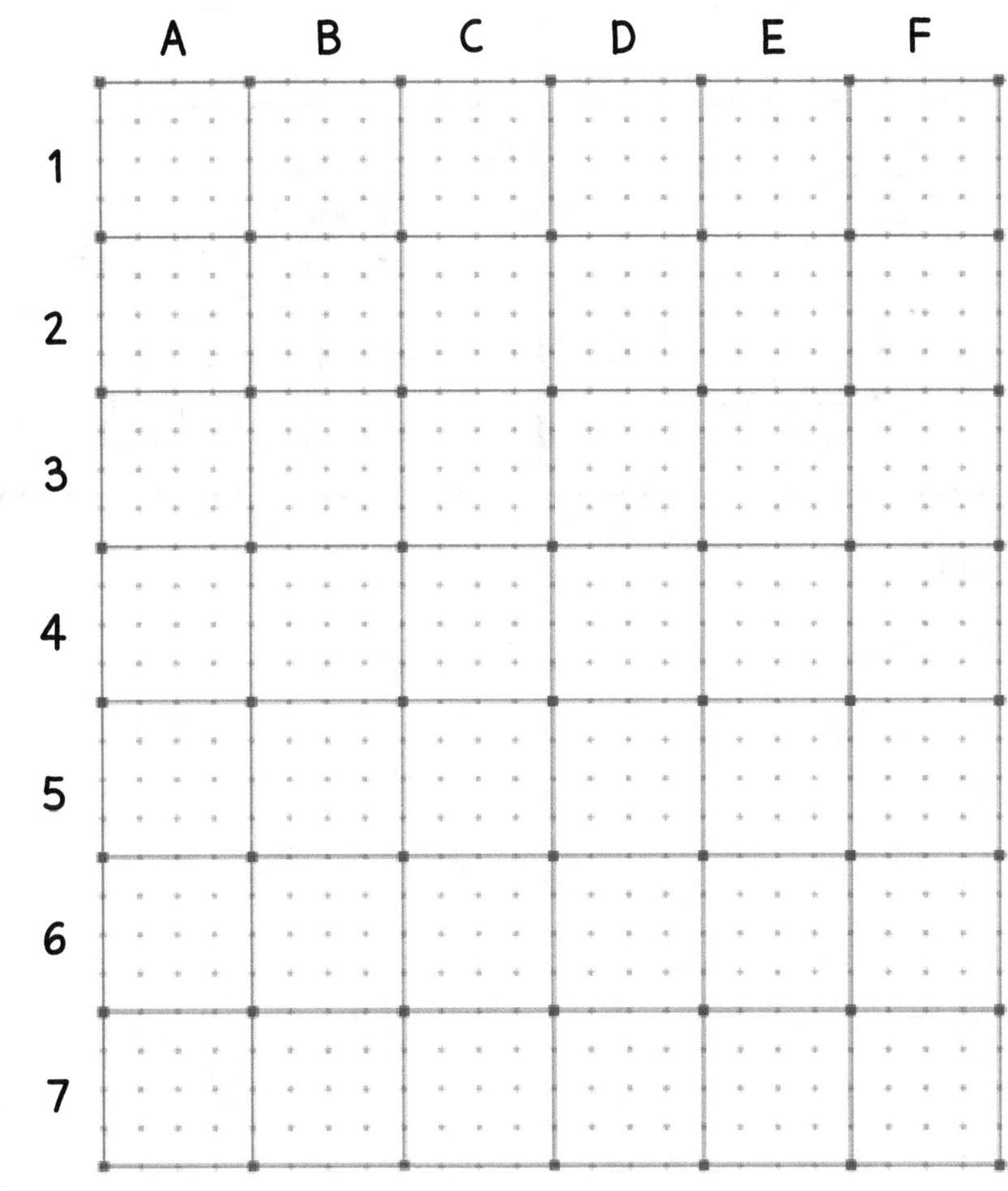

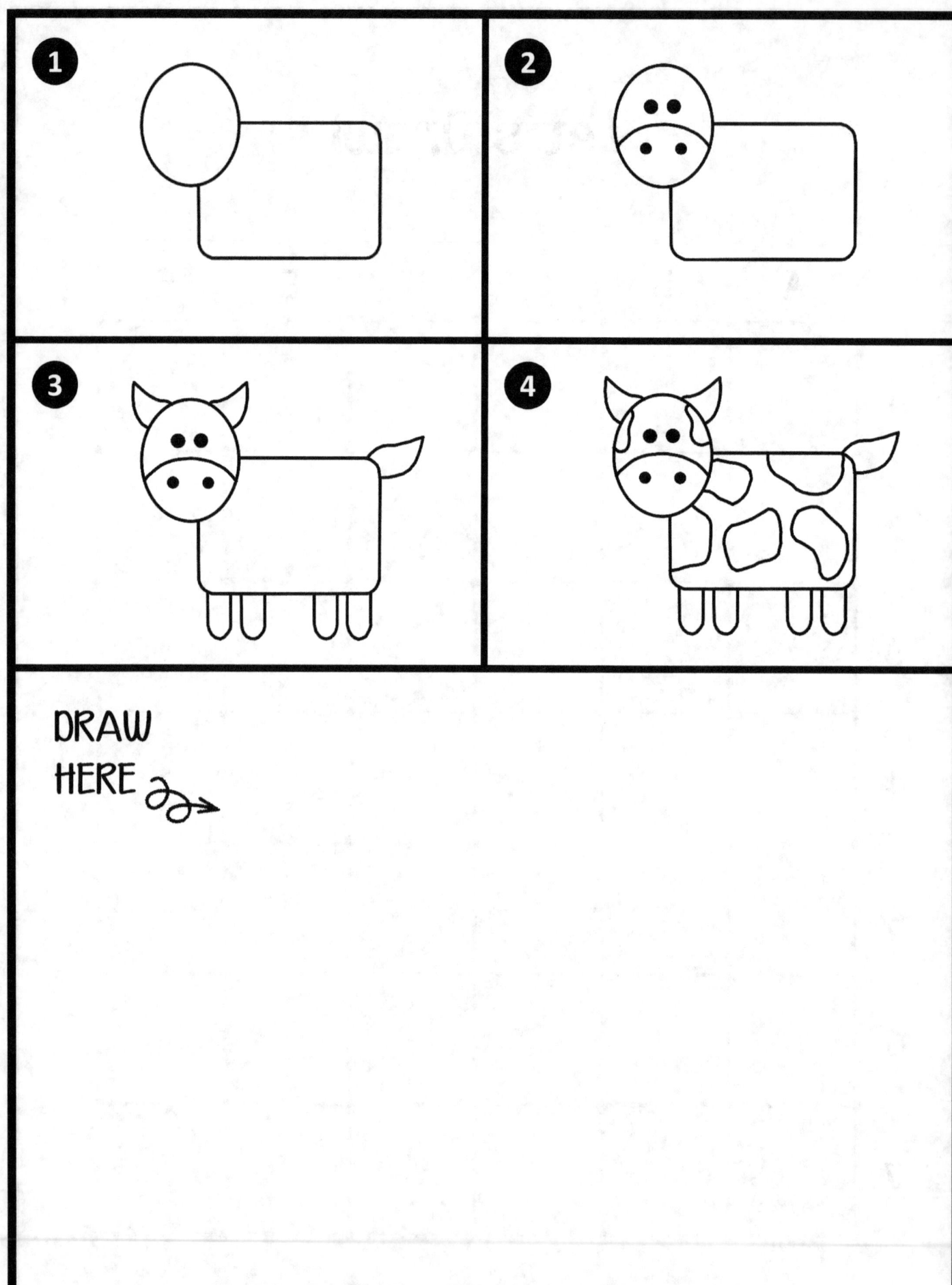

Practice

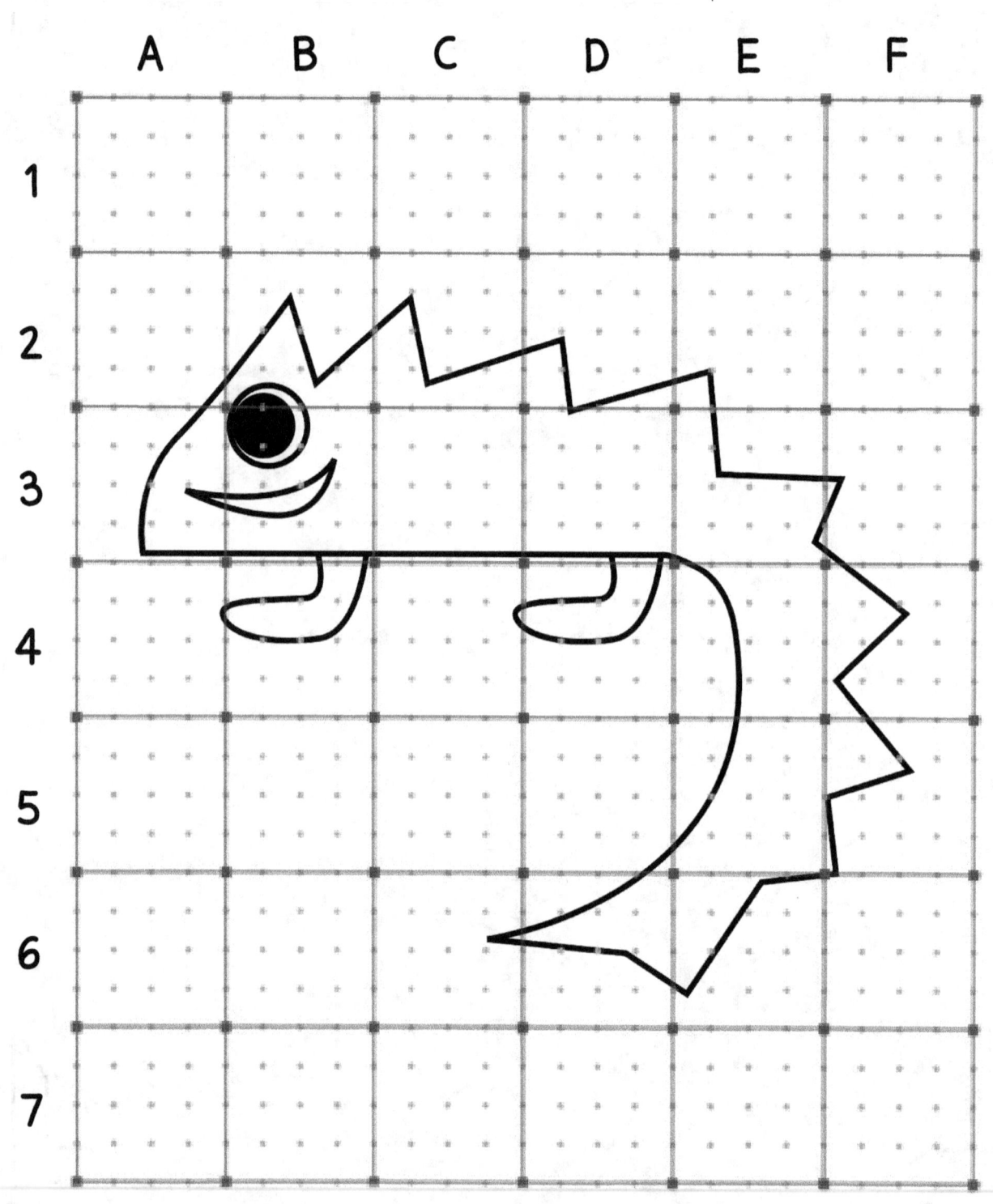

Let's Draw!

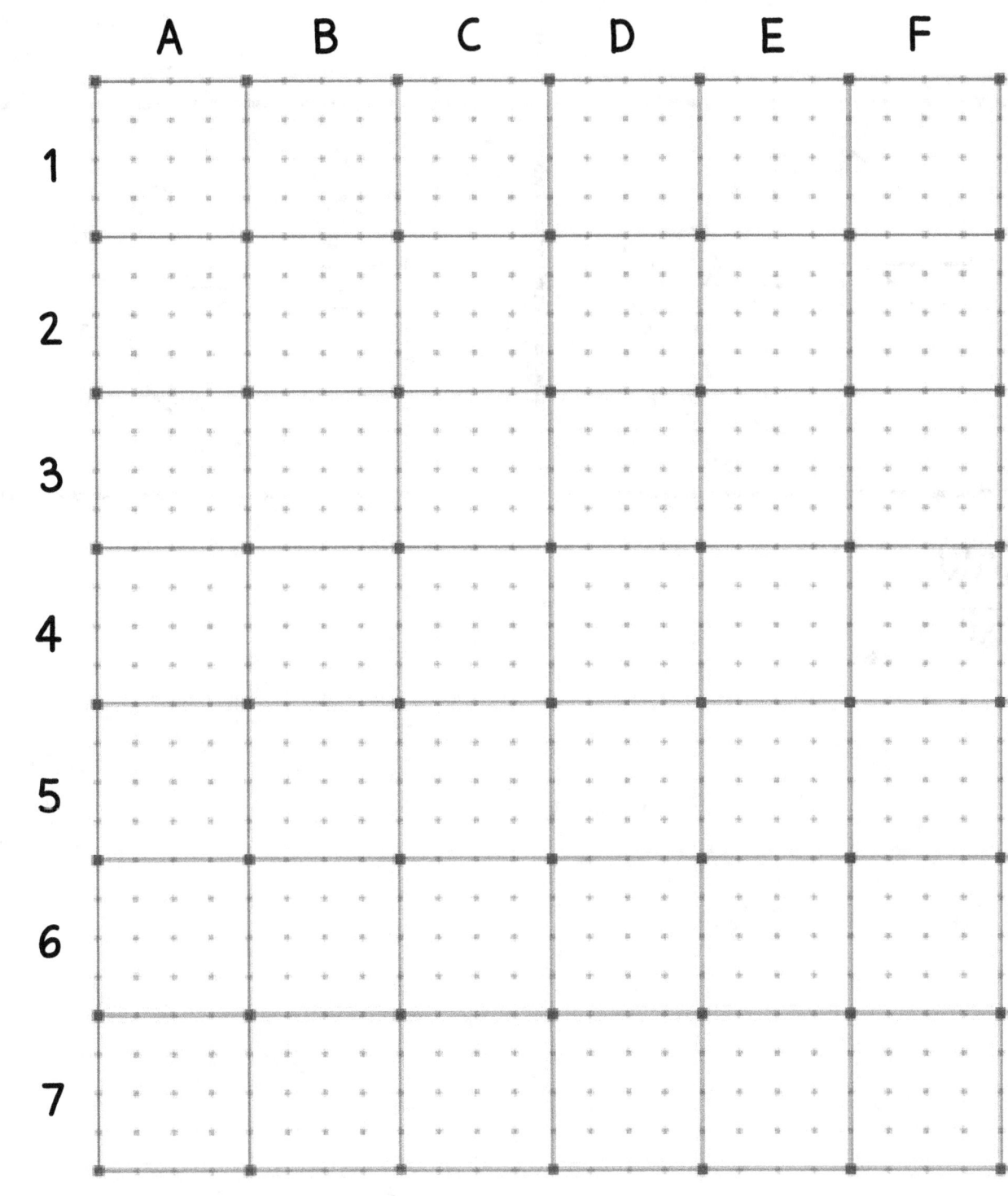

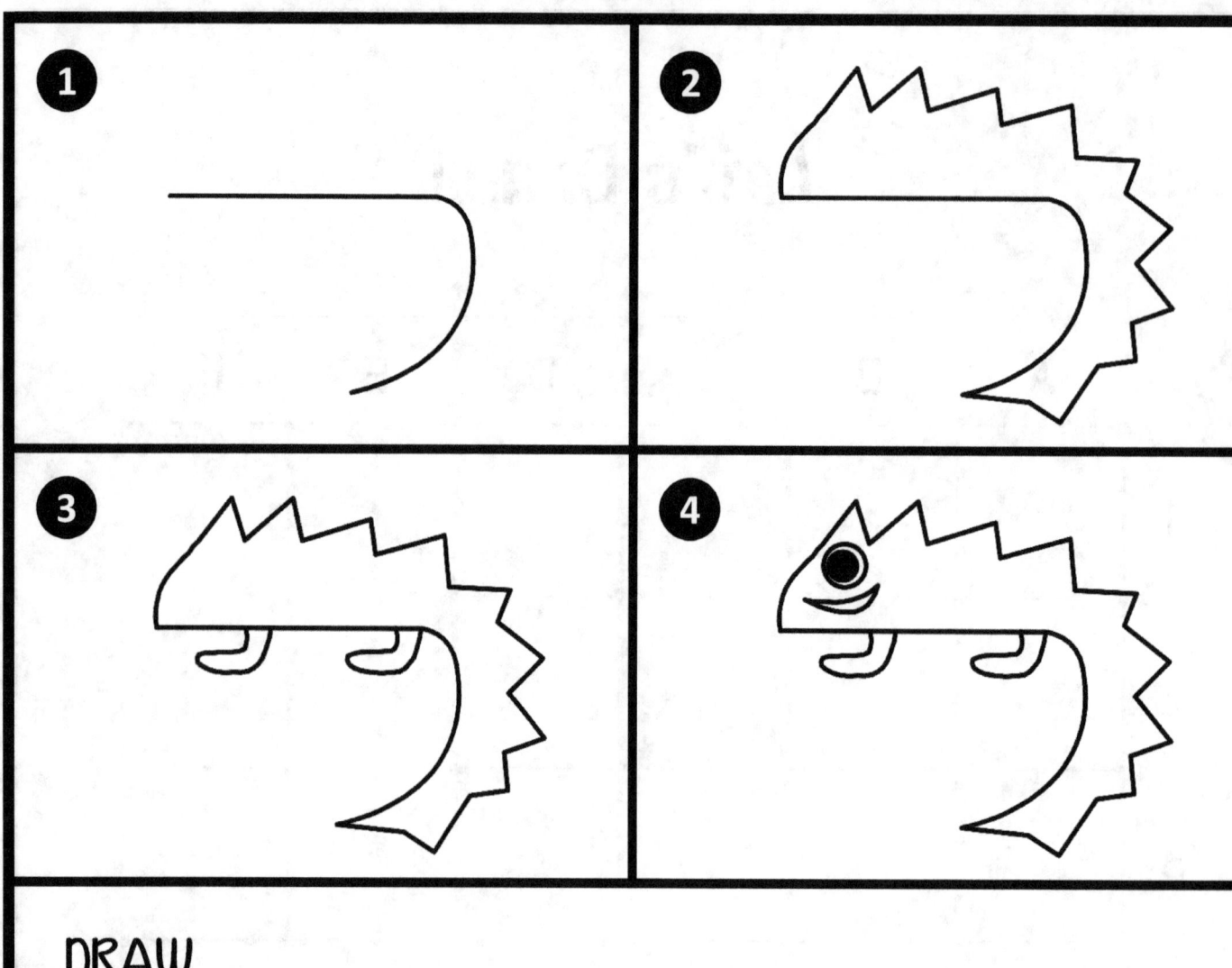

DRAW HERE

Practice

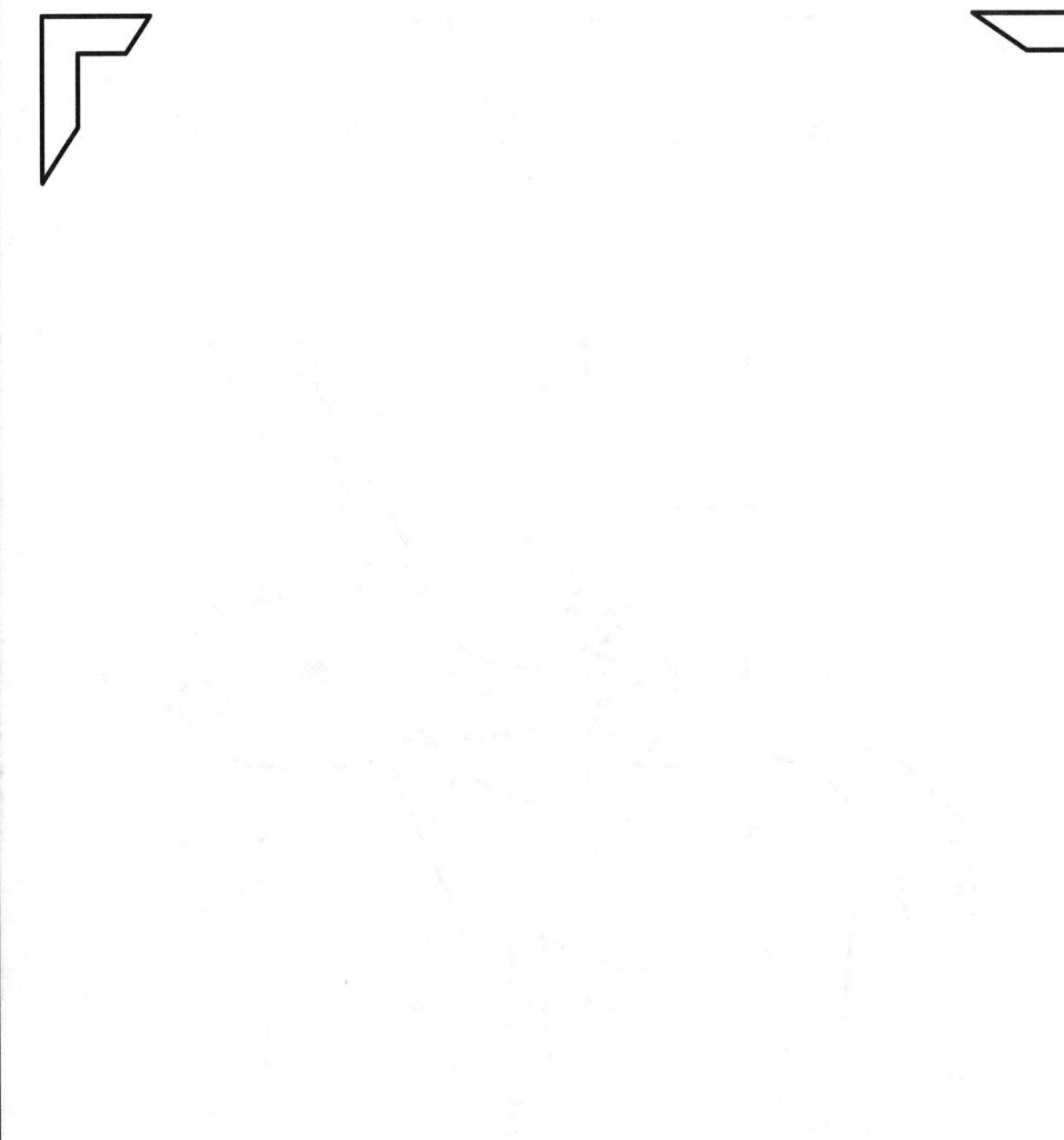

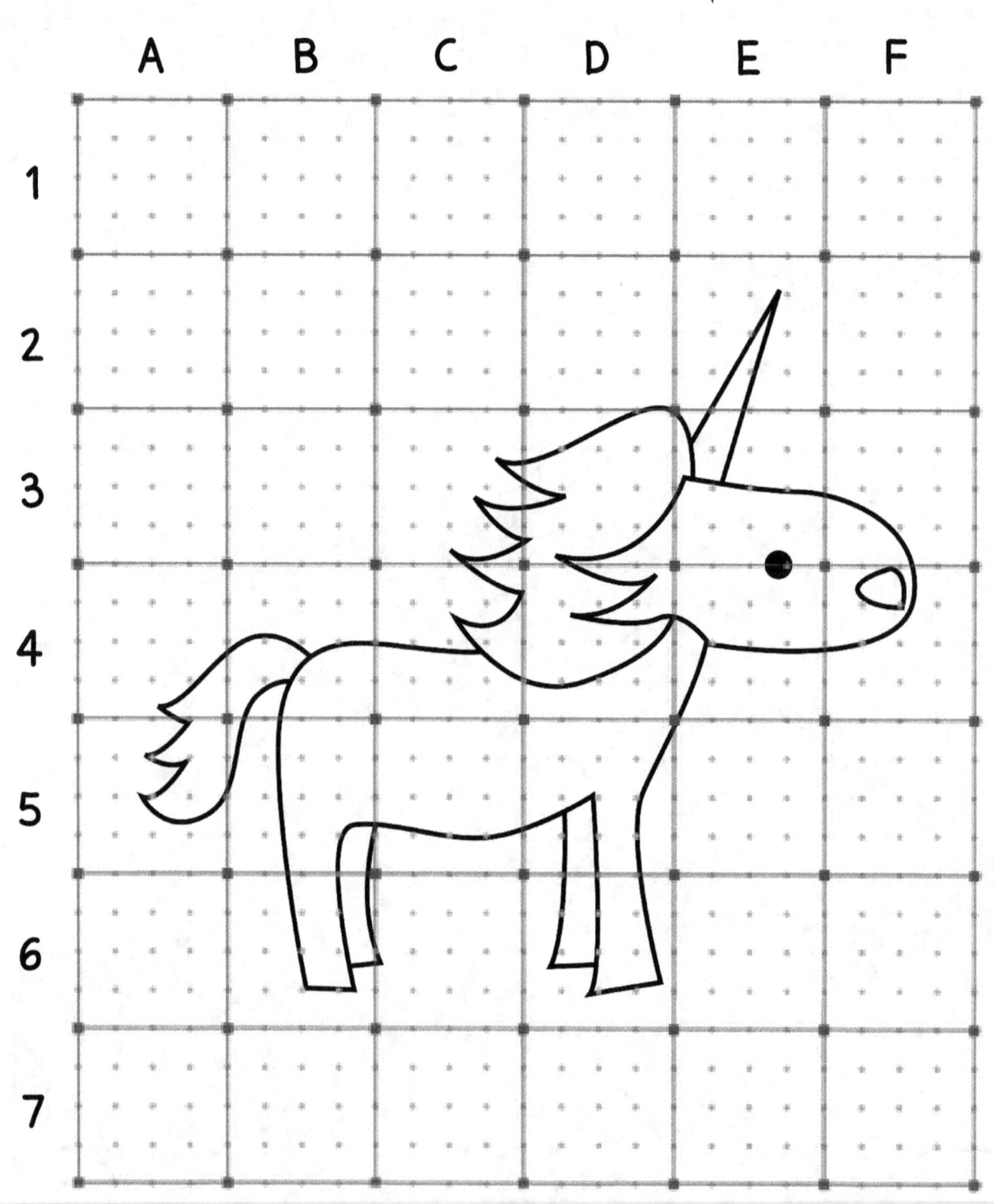

Let's Draw!

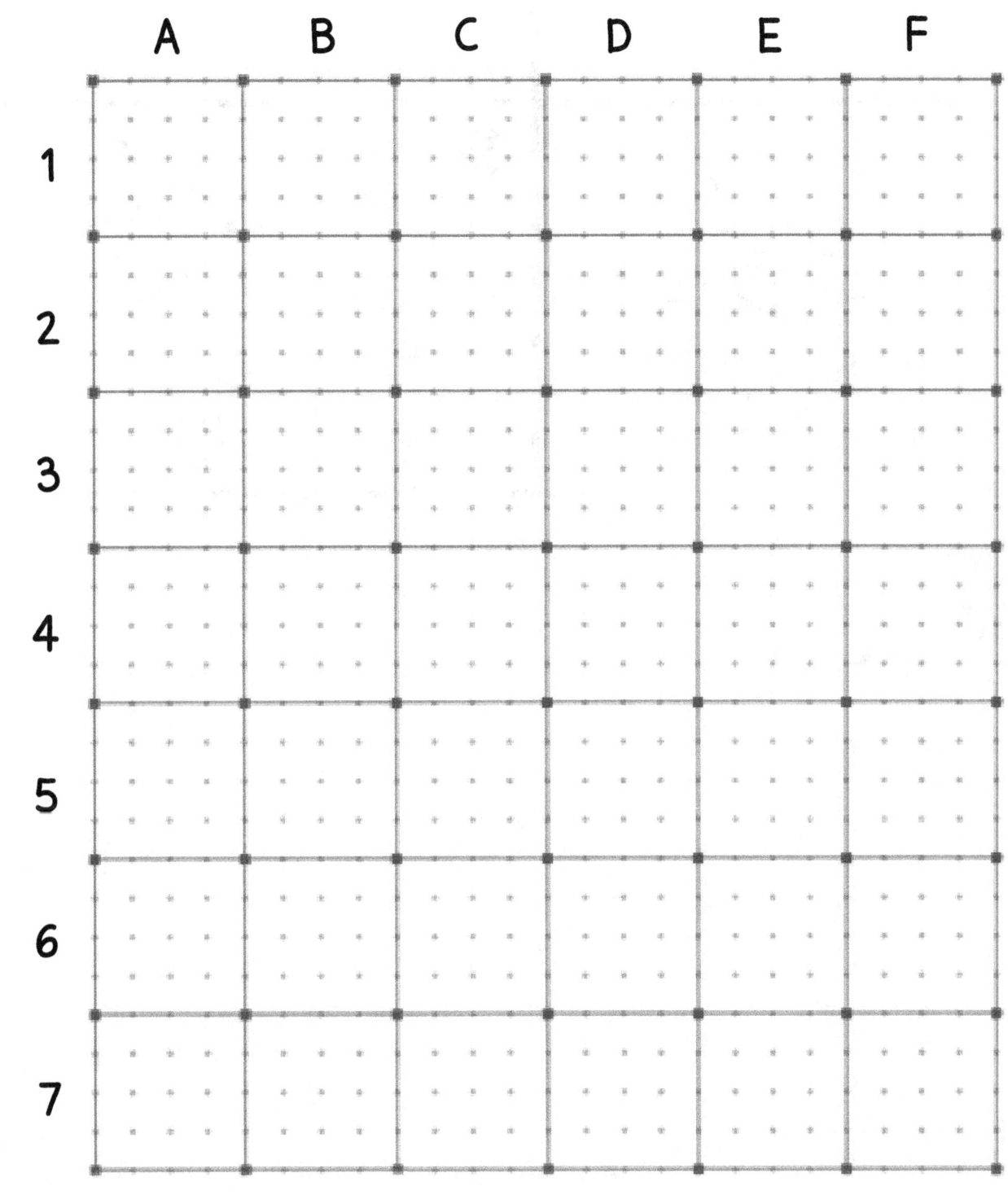

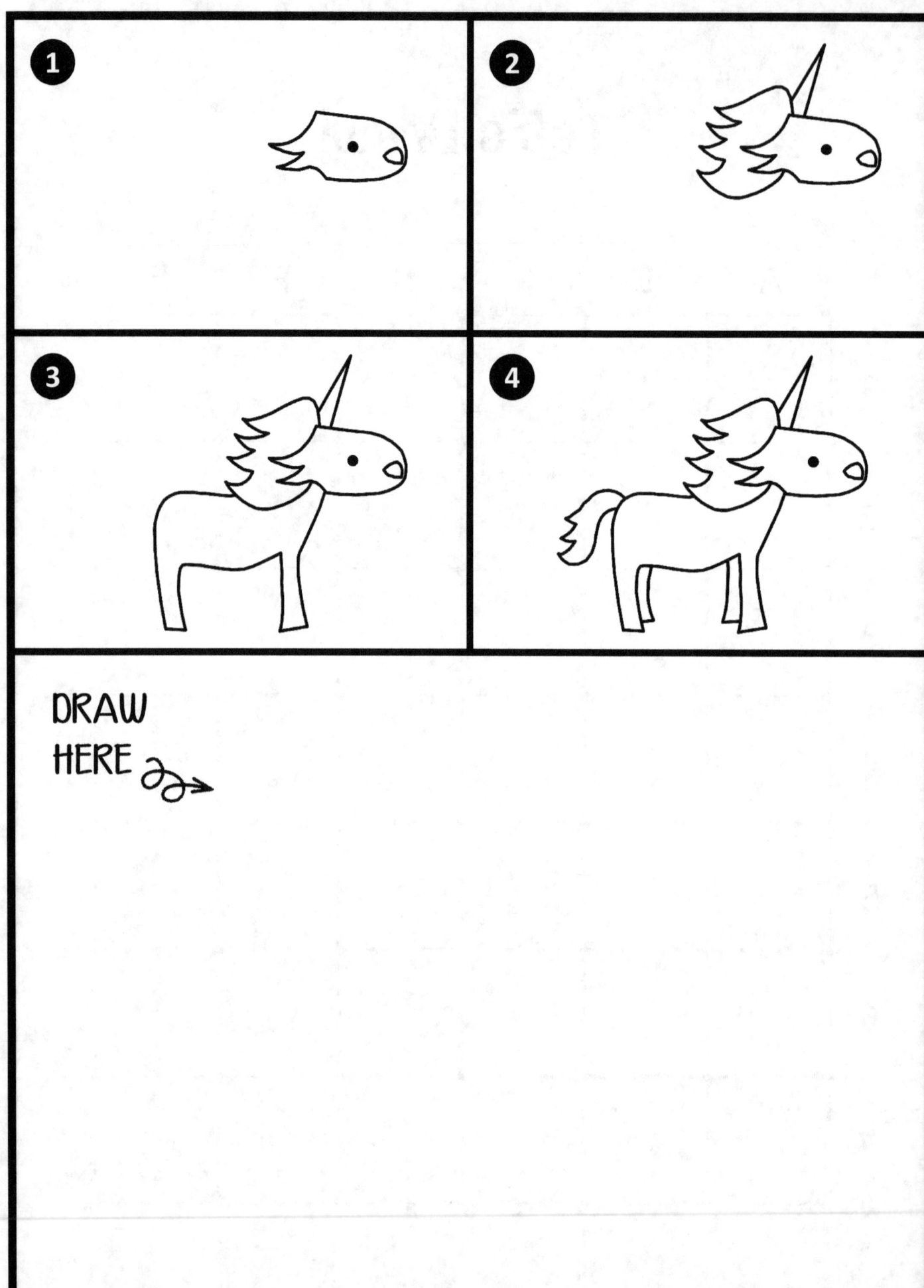

Practice

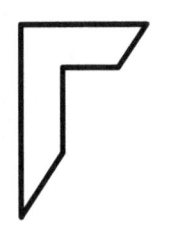
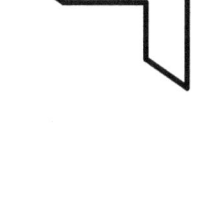
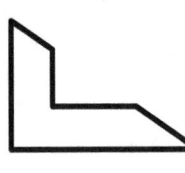
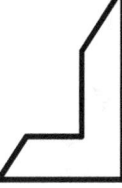

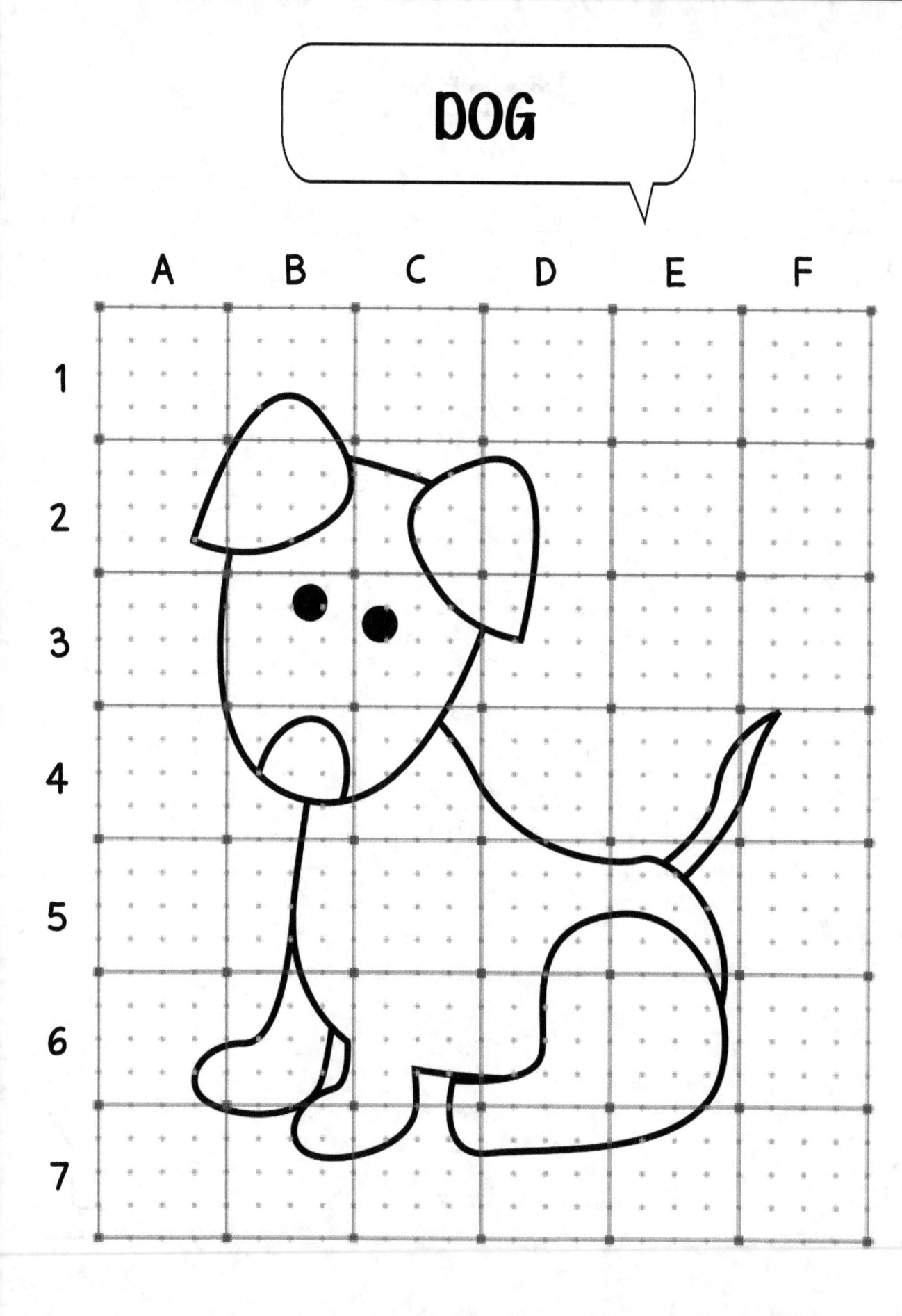

Let's Draw!

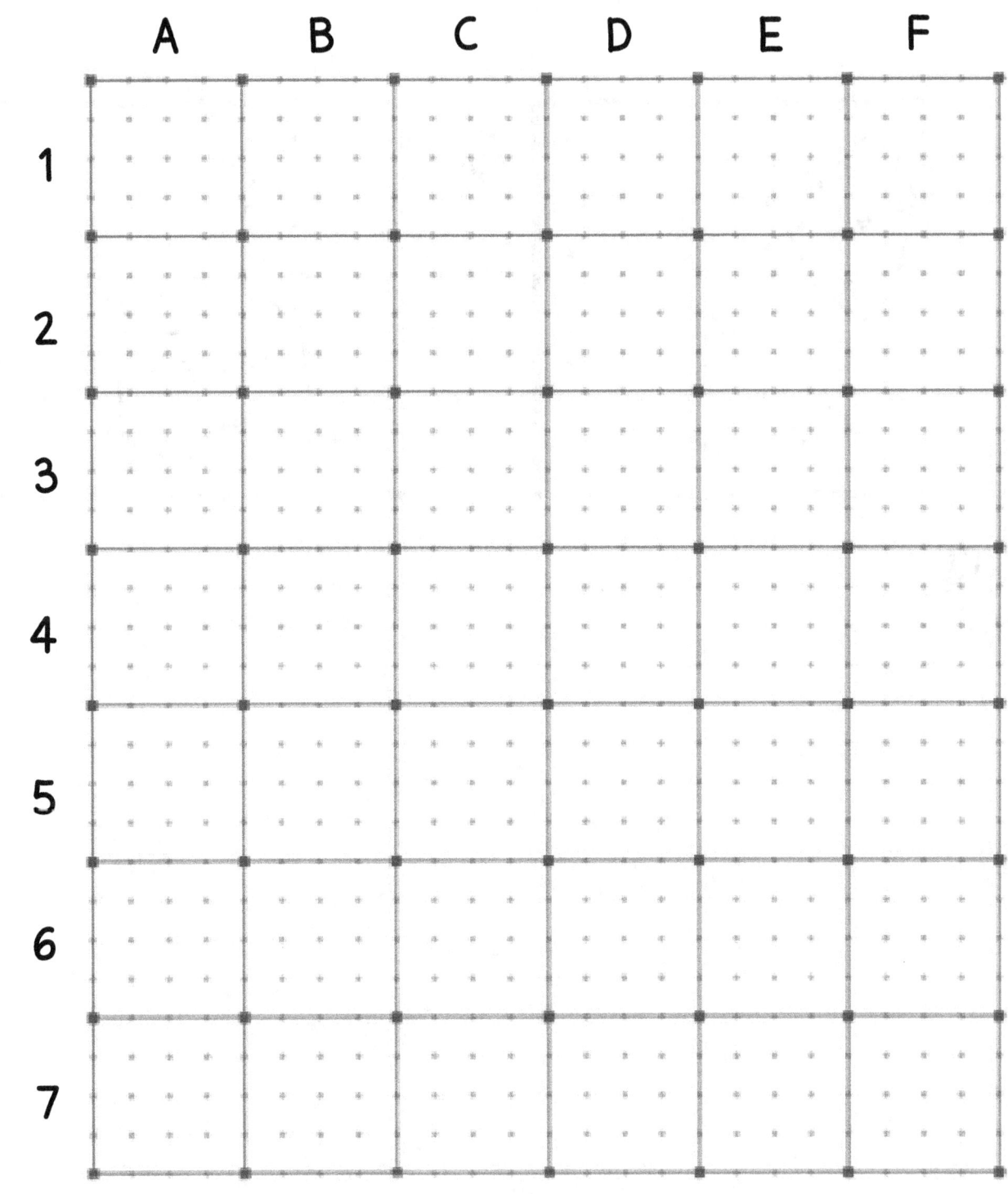

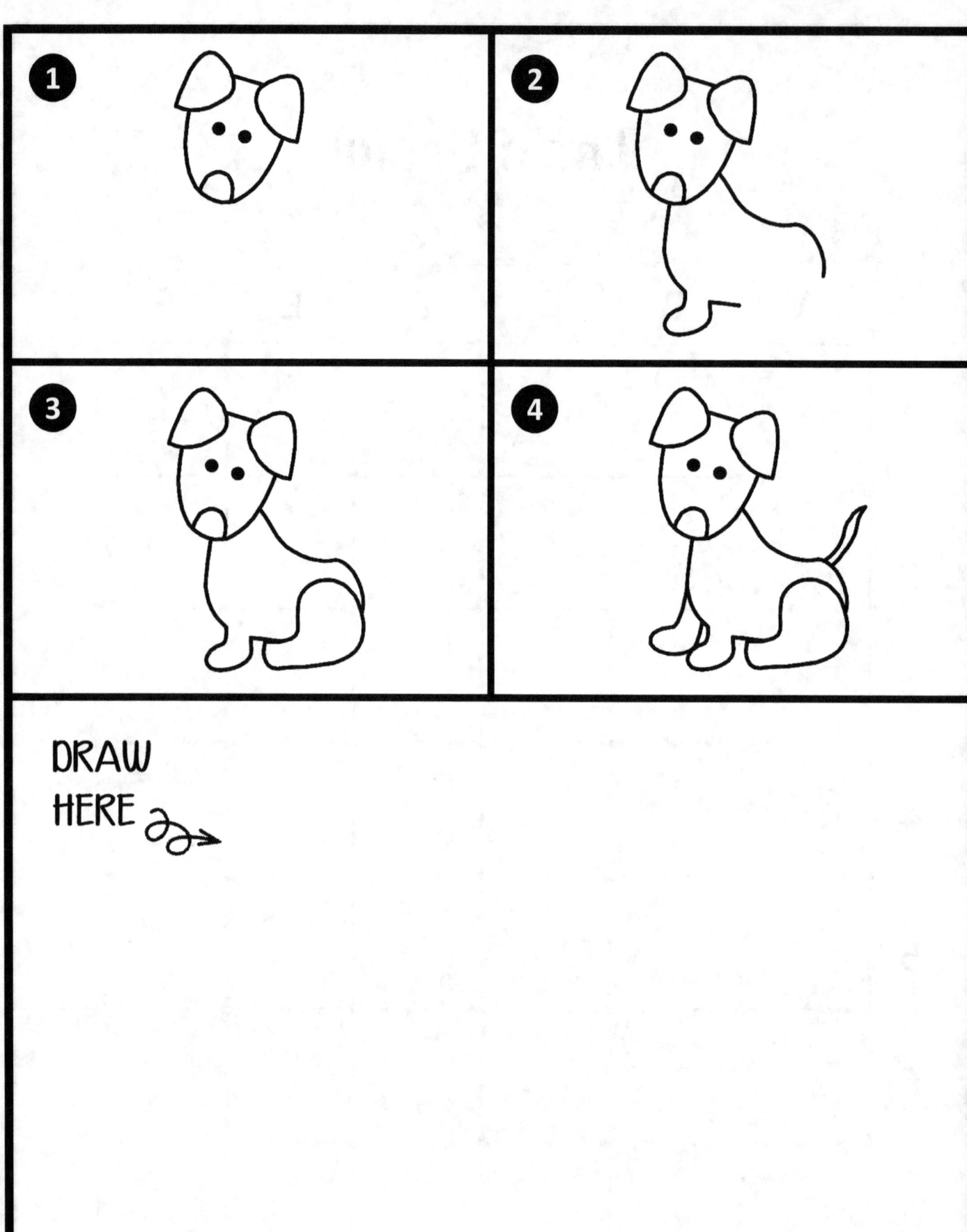

Practice

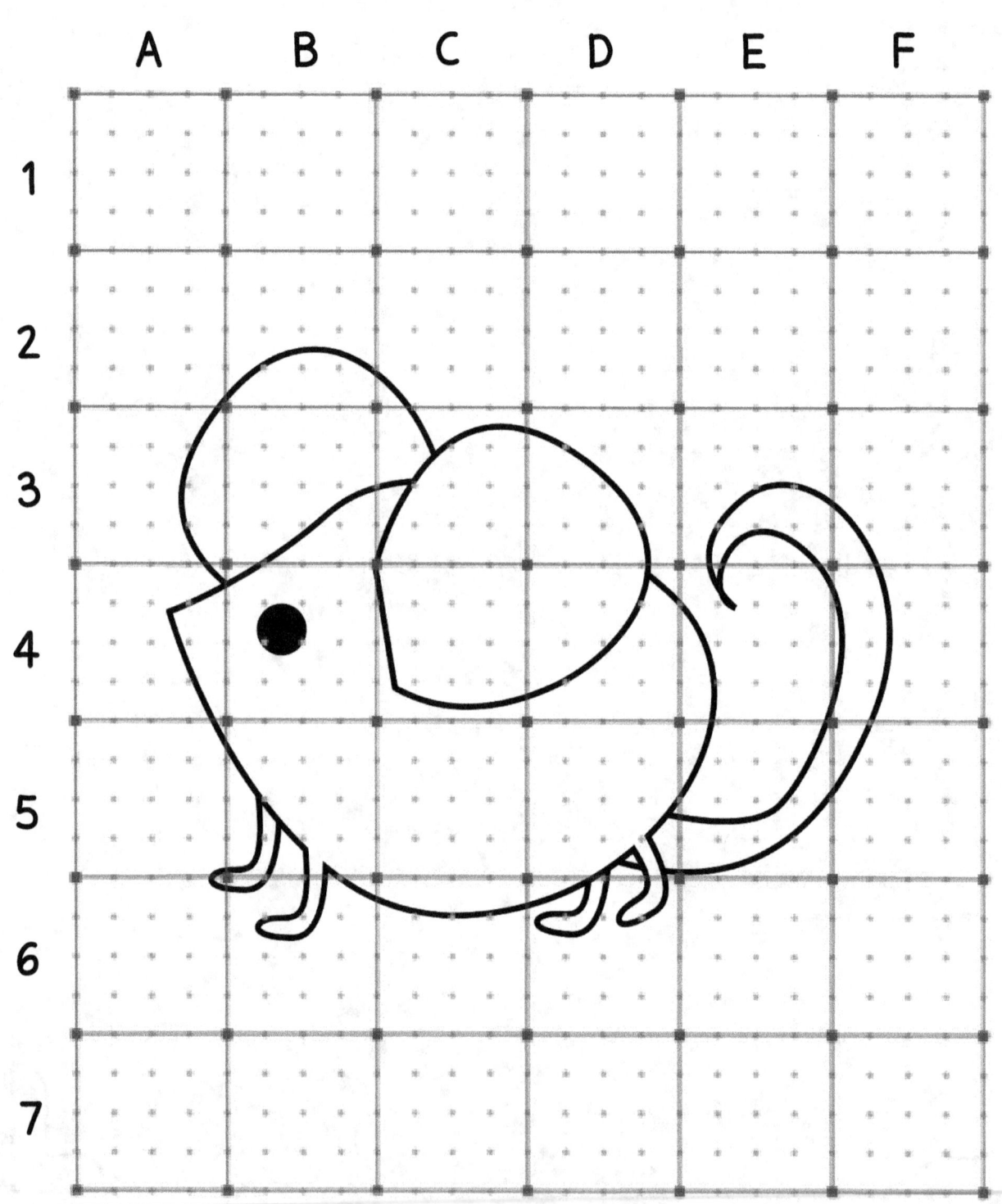

Let's Draw!

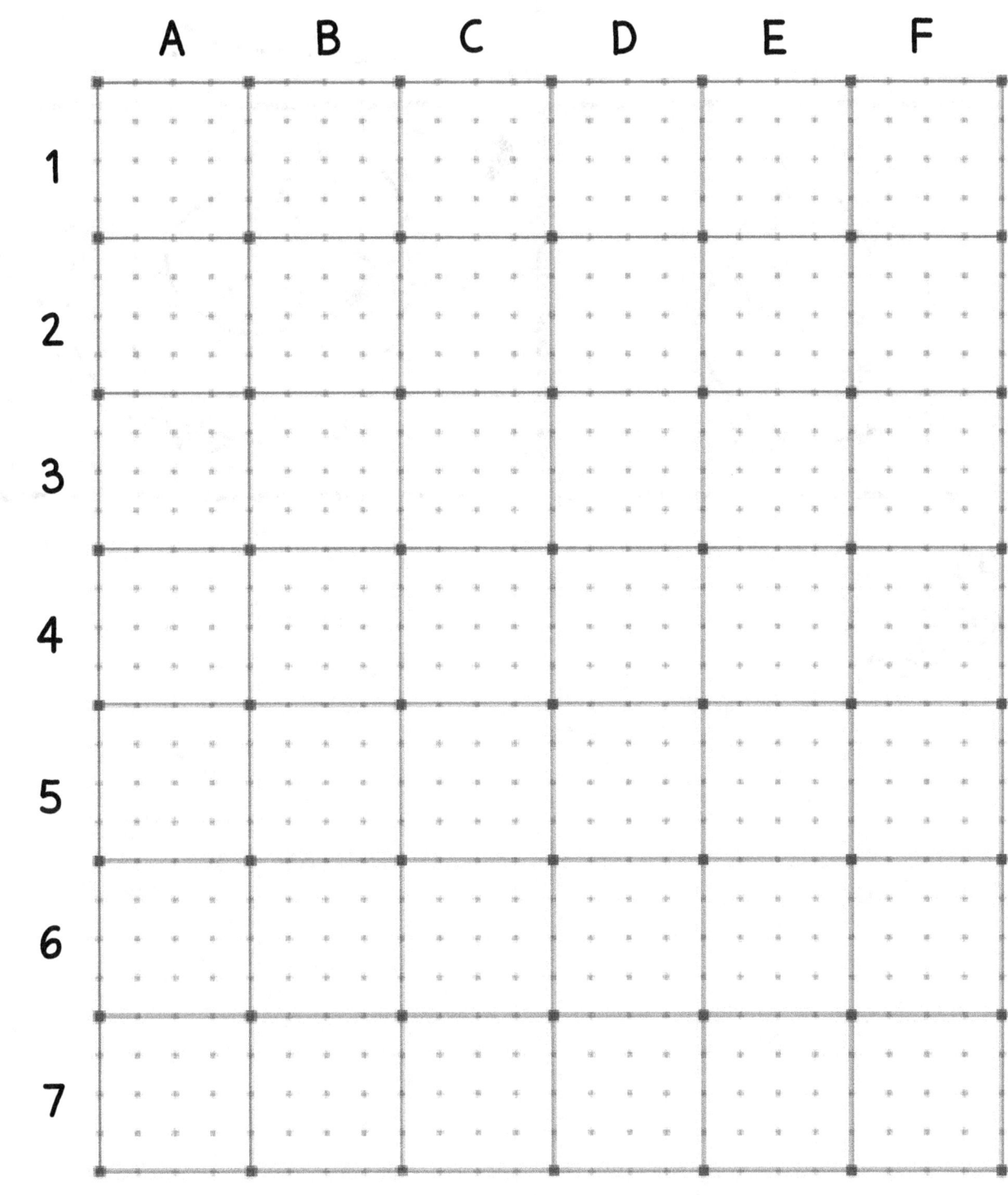

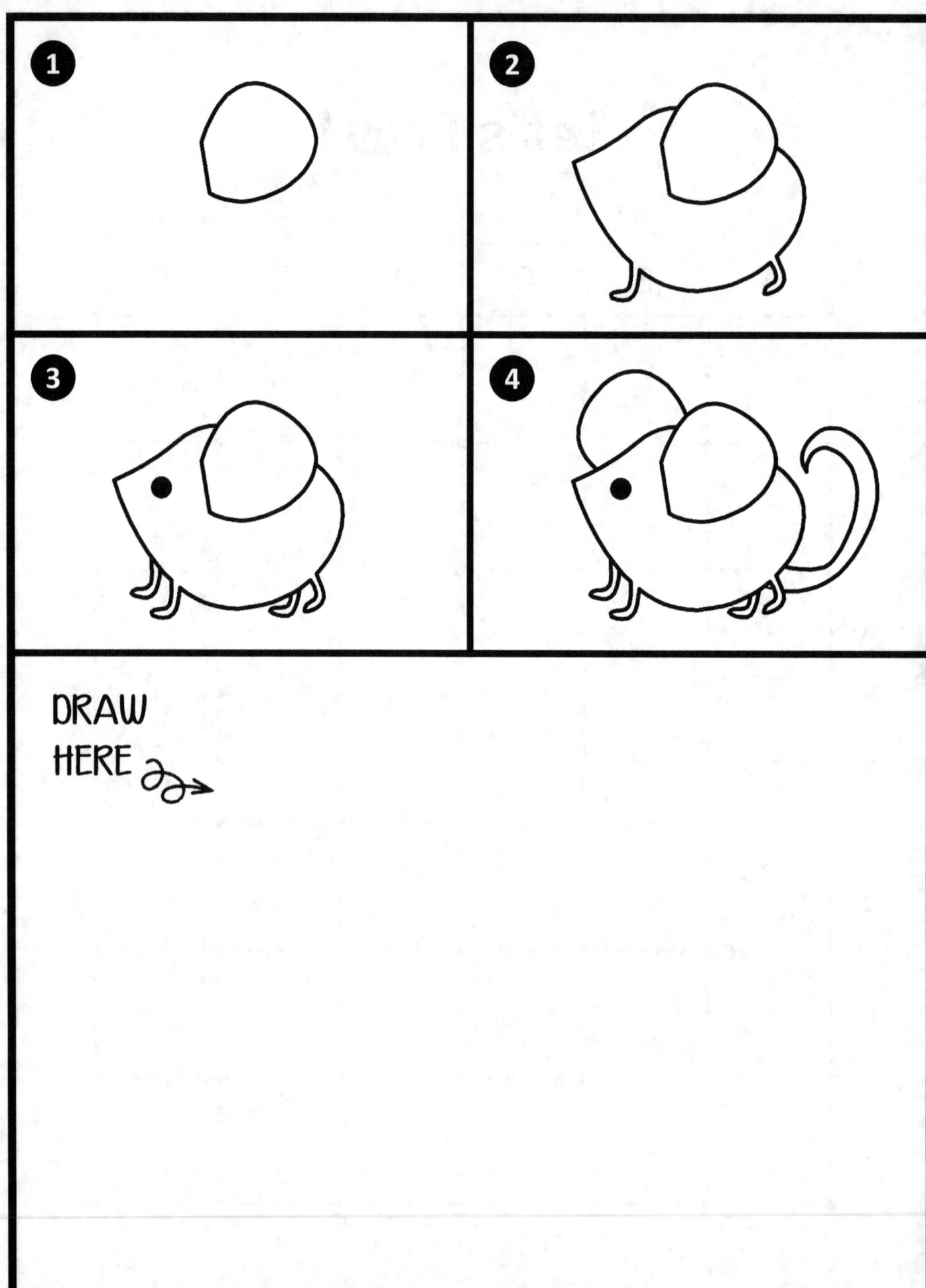

Practice

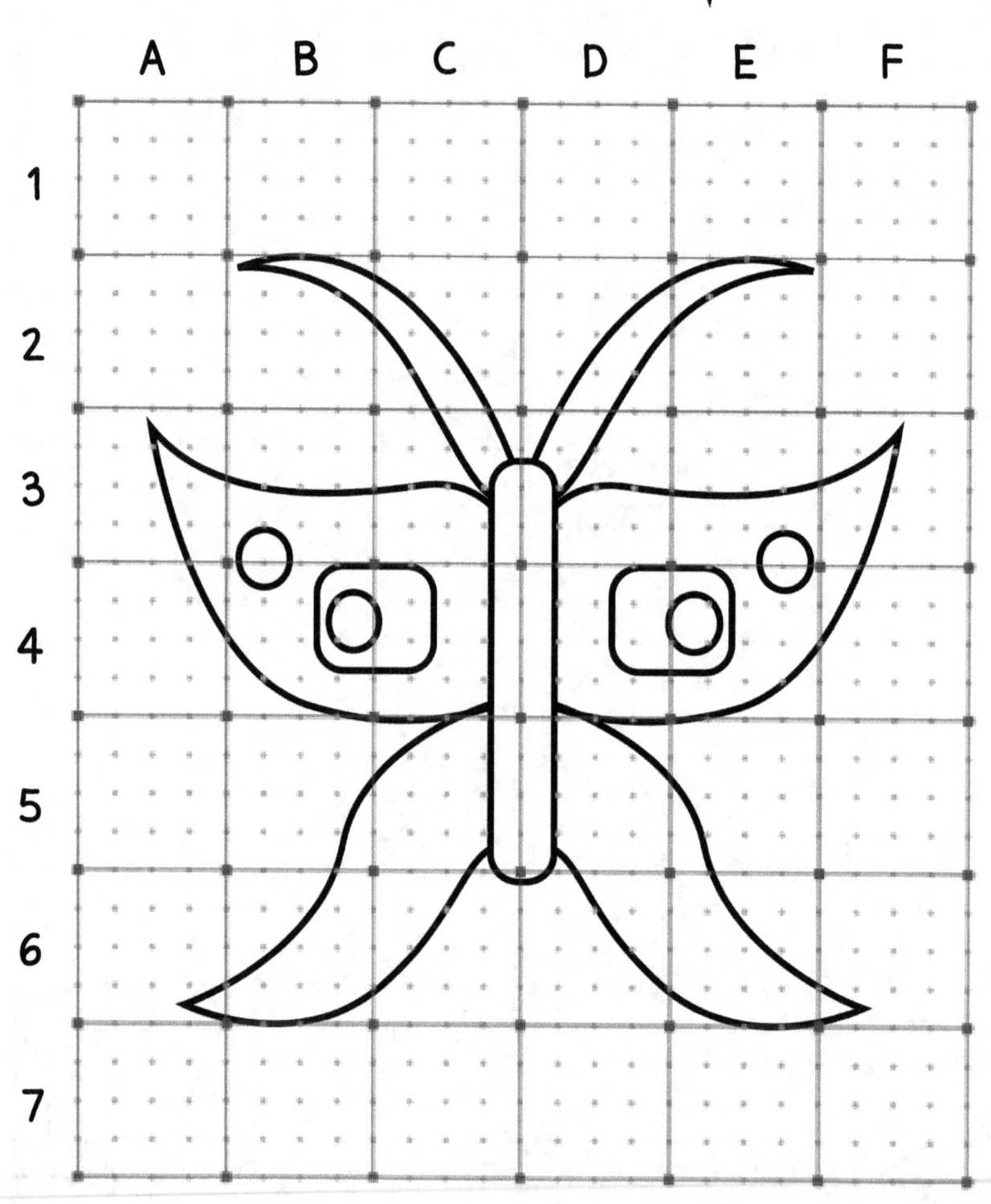

Let's Draw!

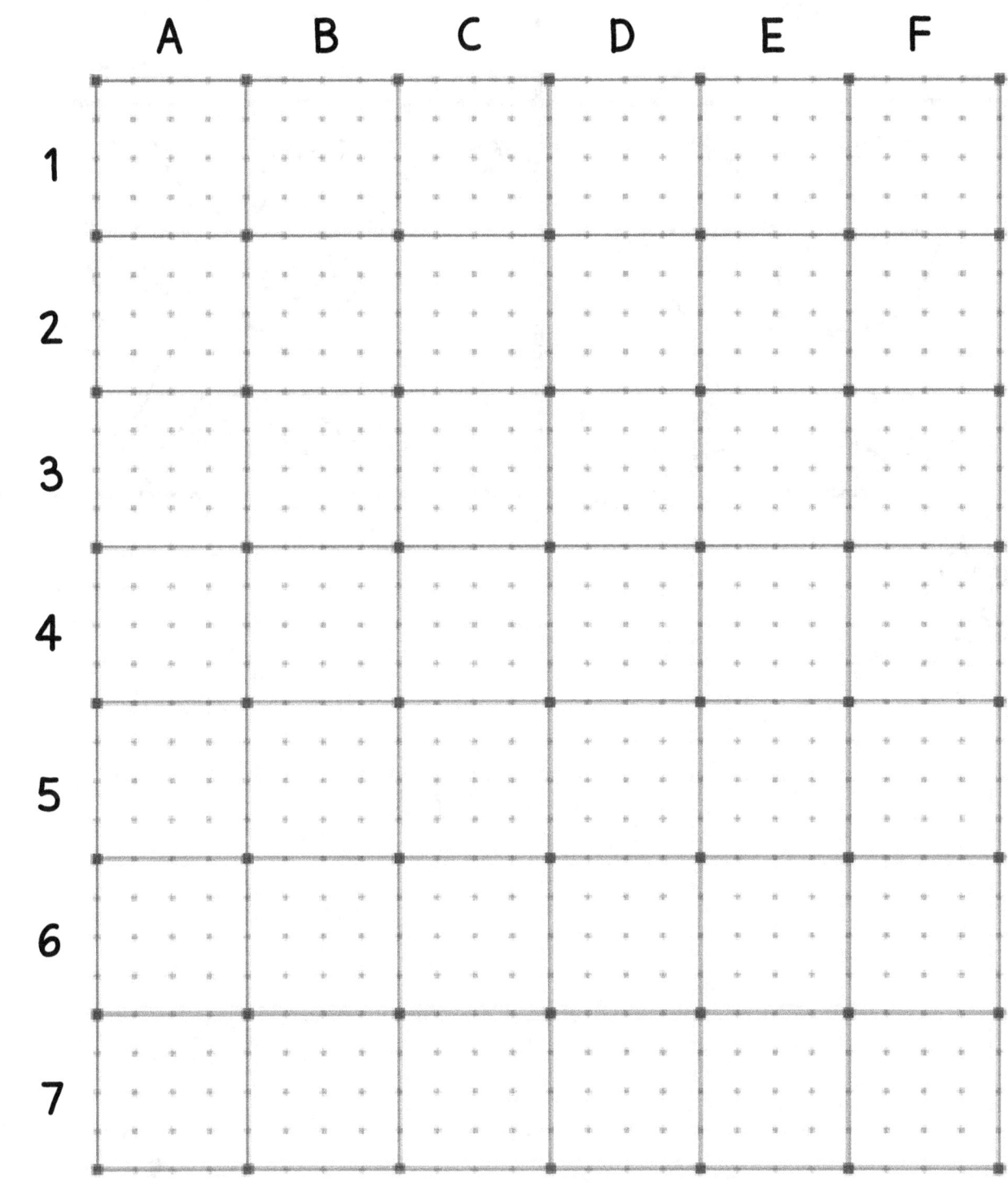

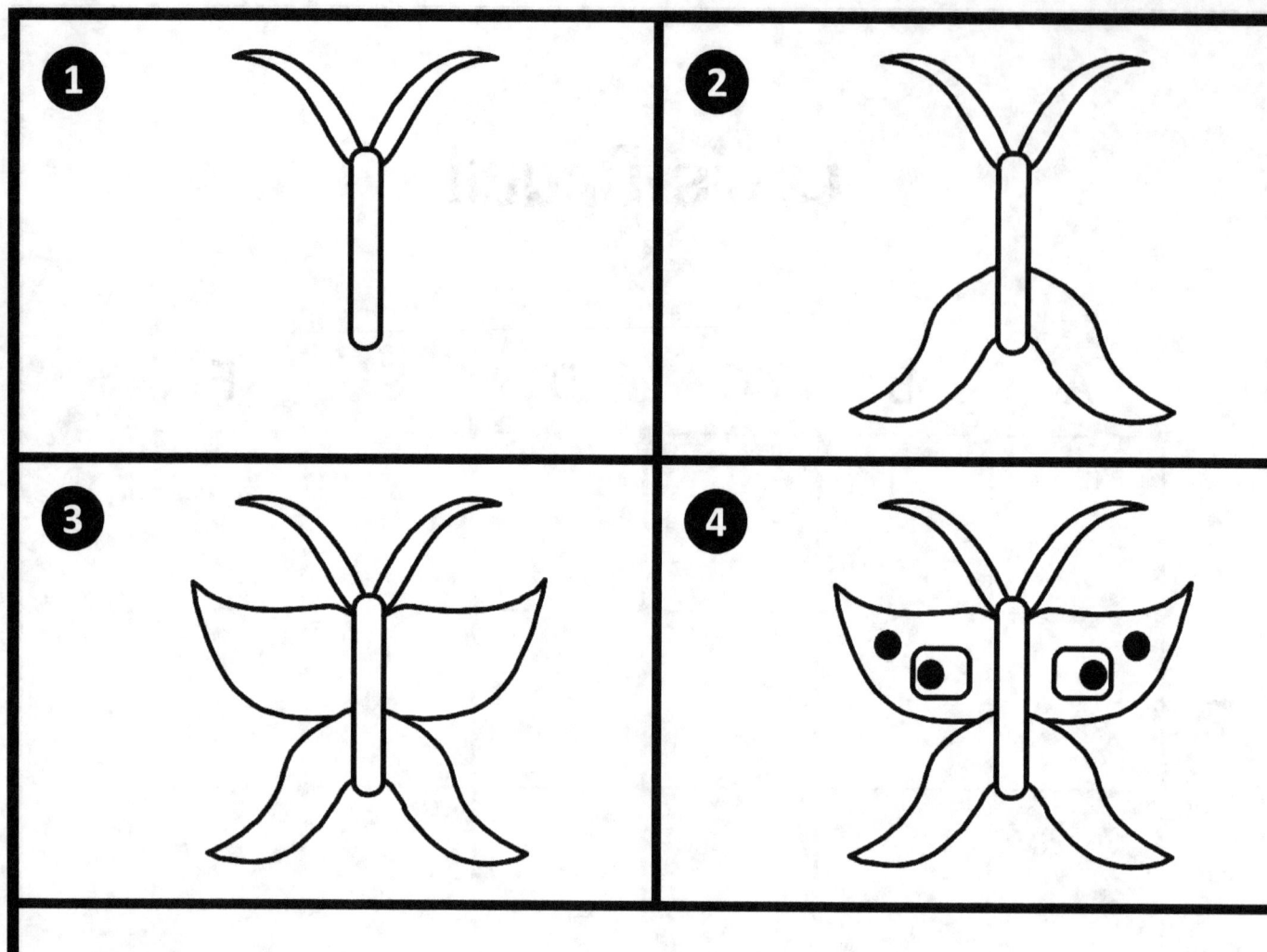

DRAW HERE

Practice

MONKEY

	A	B	C	D	E	F
1						
2						
3						
4						
5						
6						
7						

Let's Draw!

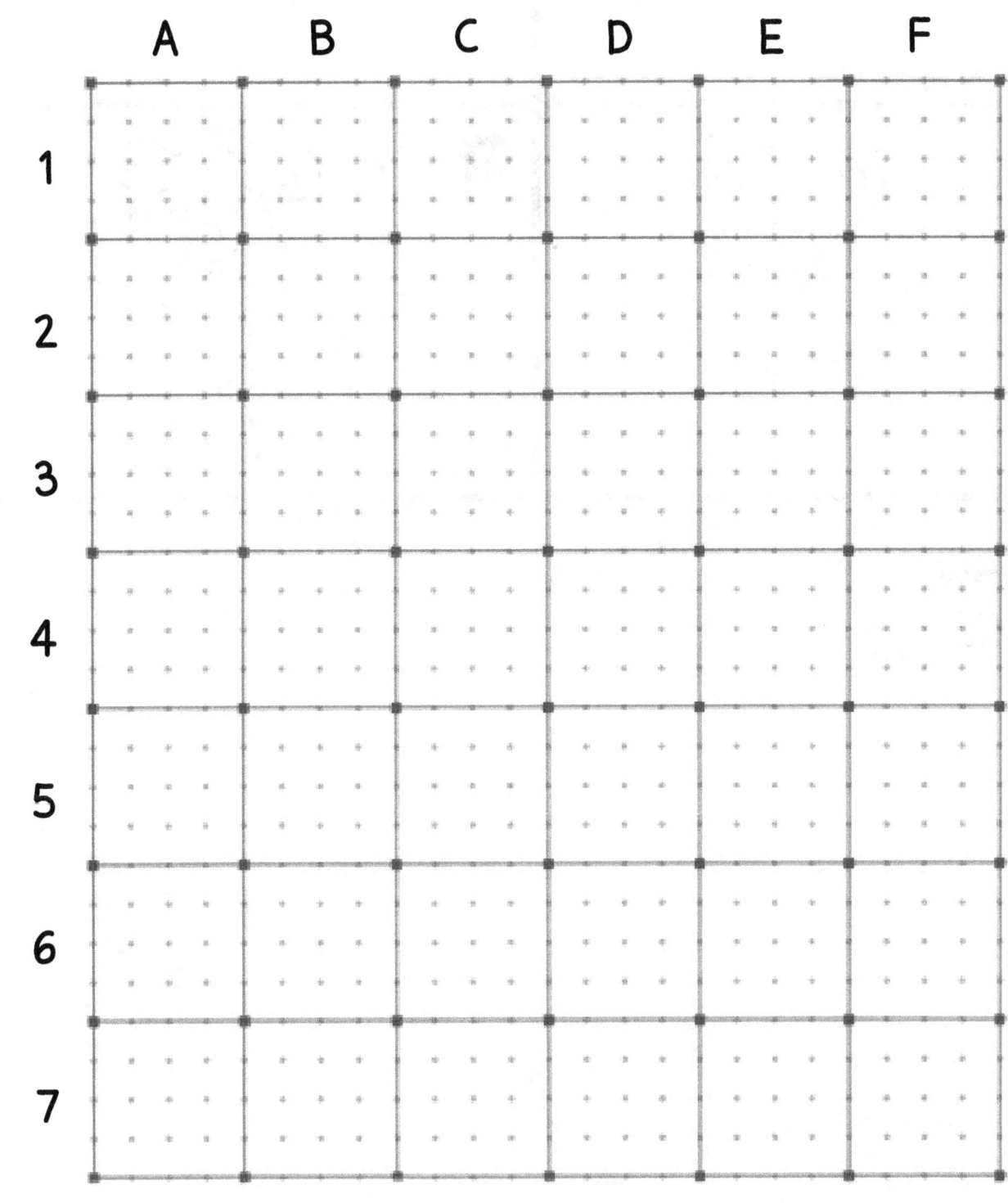

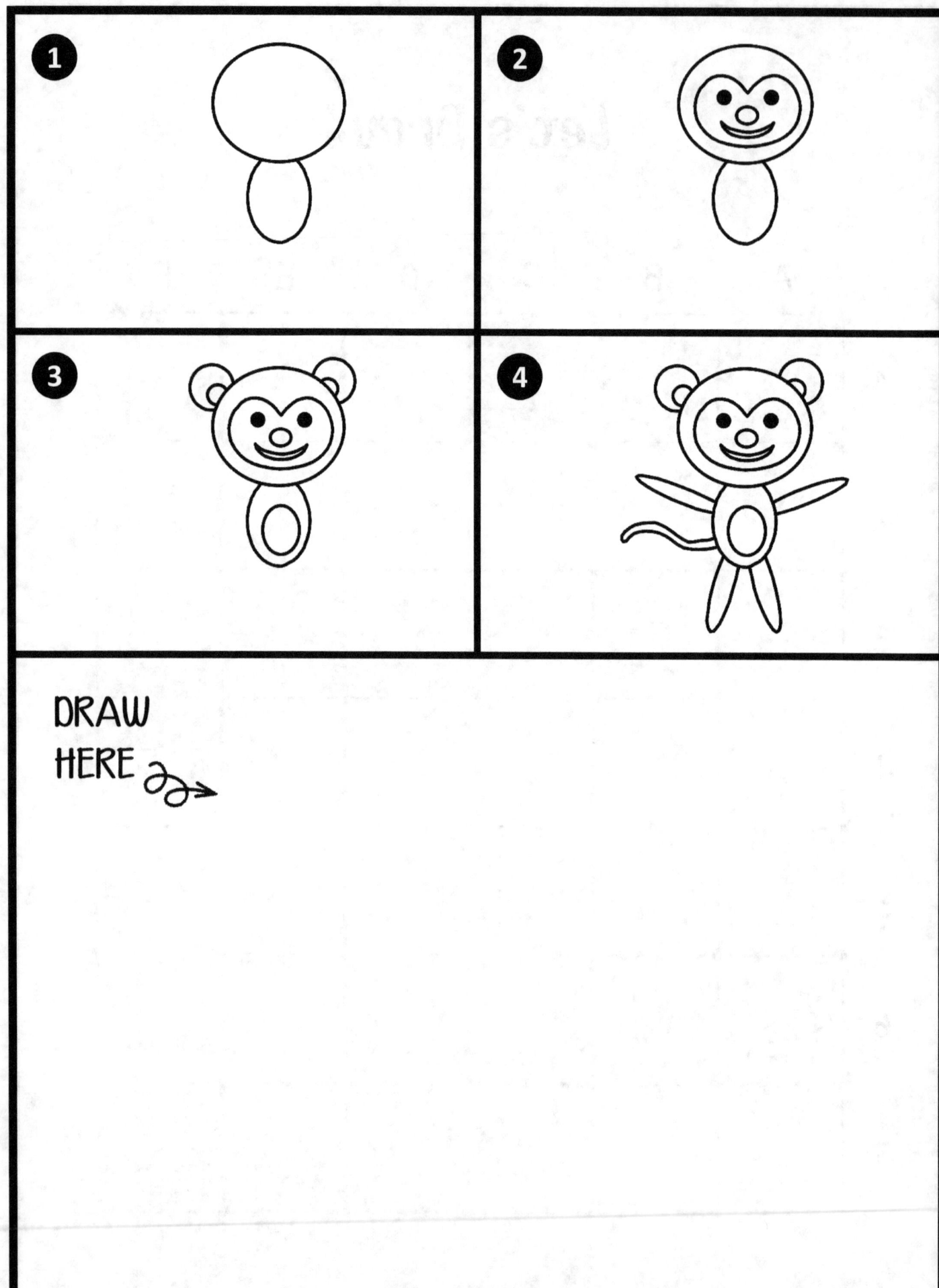

Practice

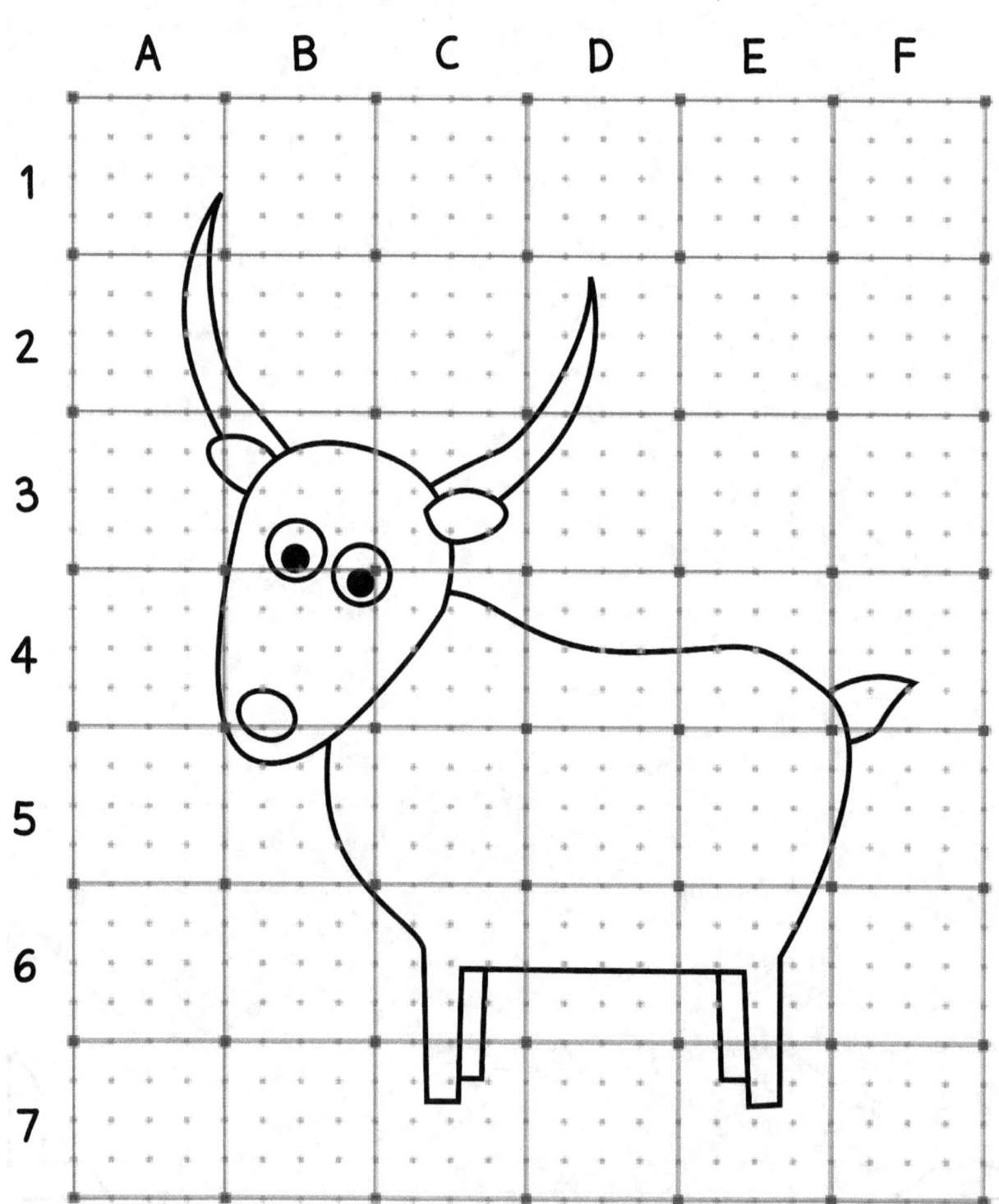

Let's Draw!

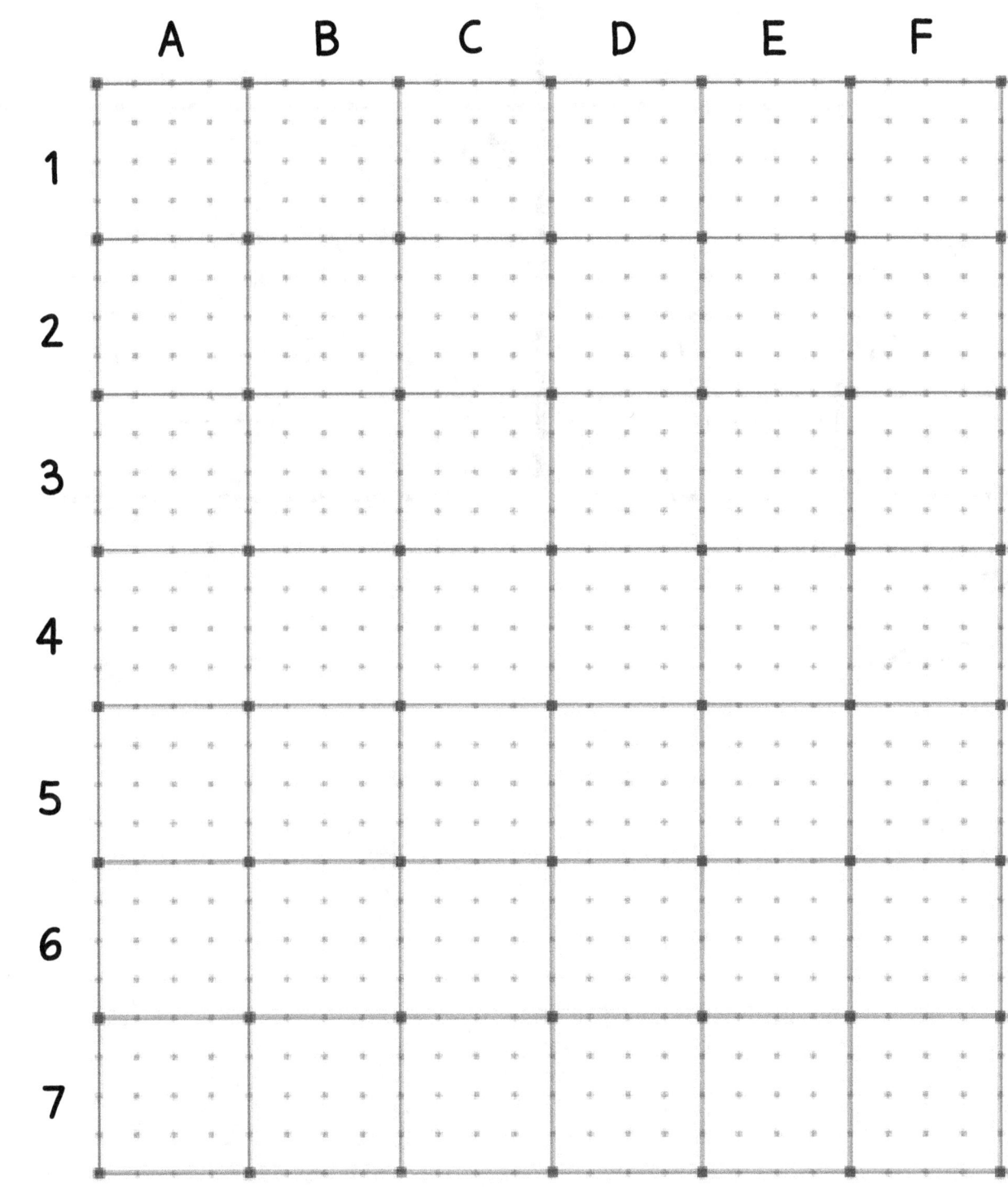

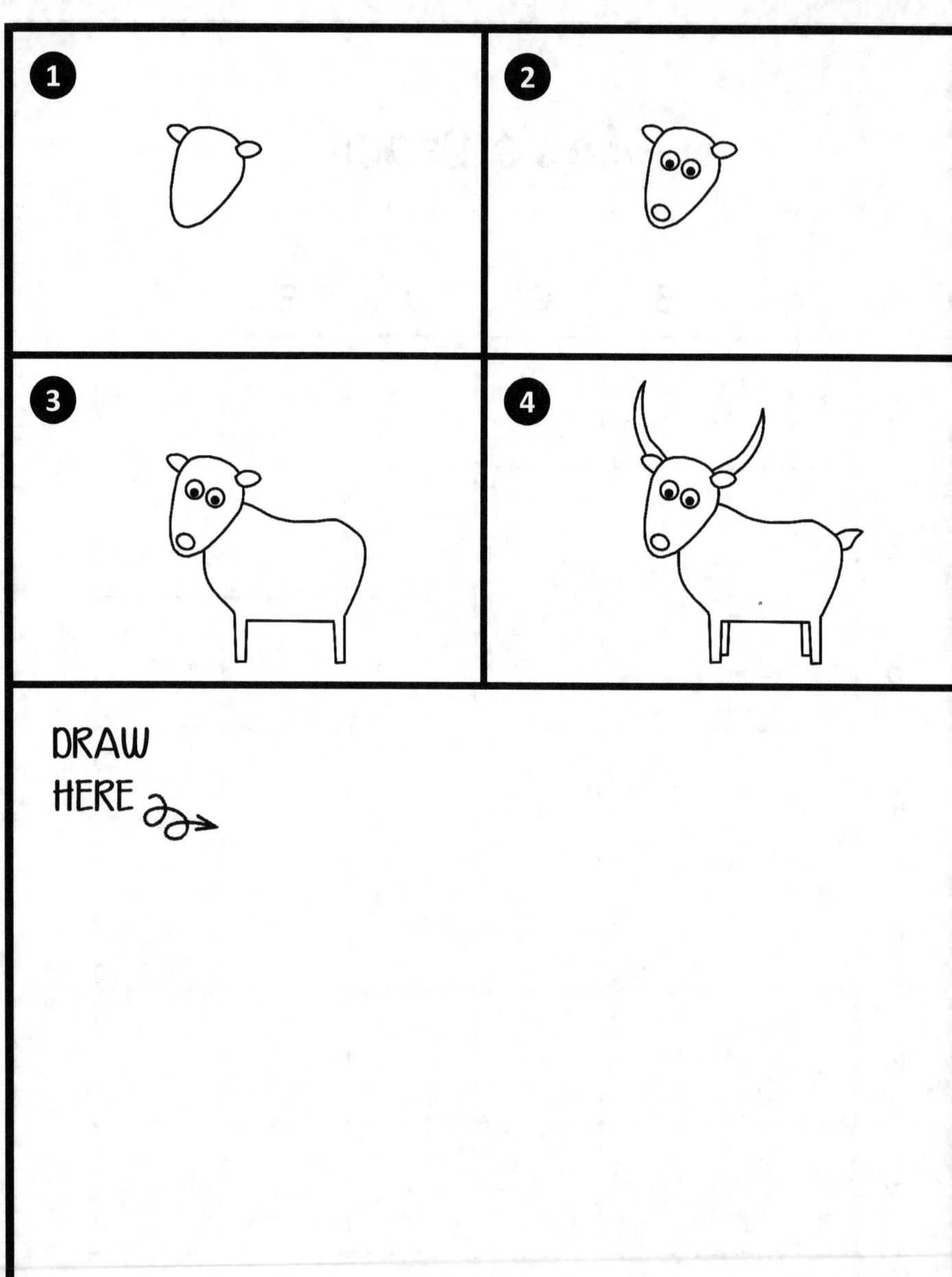

Practice

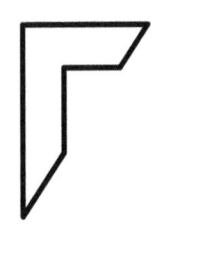
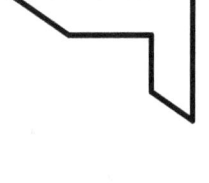
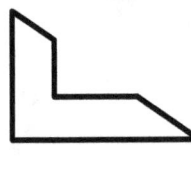
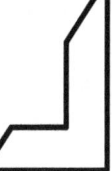

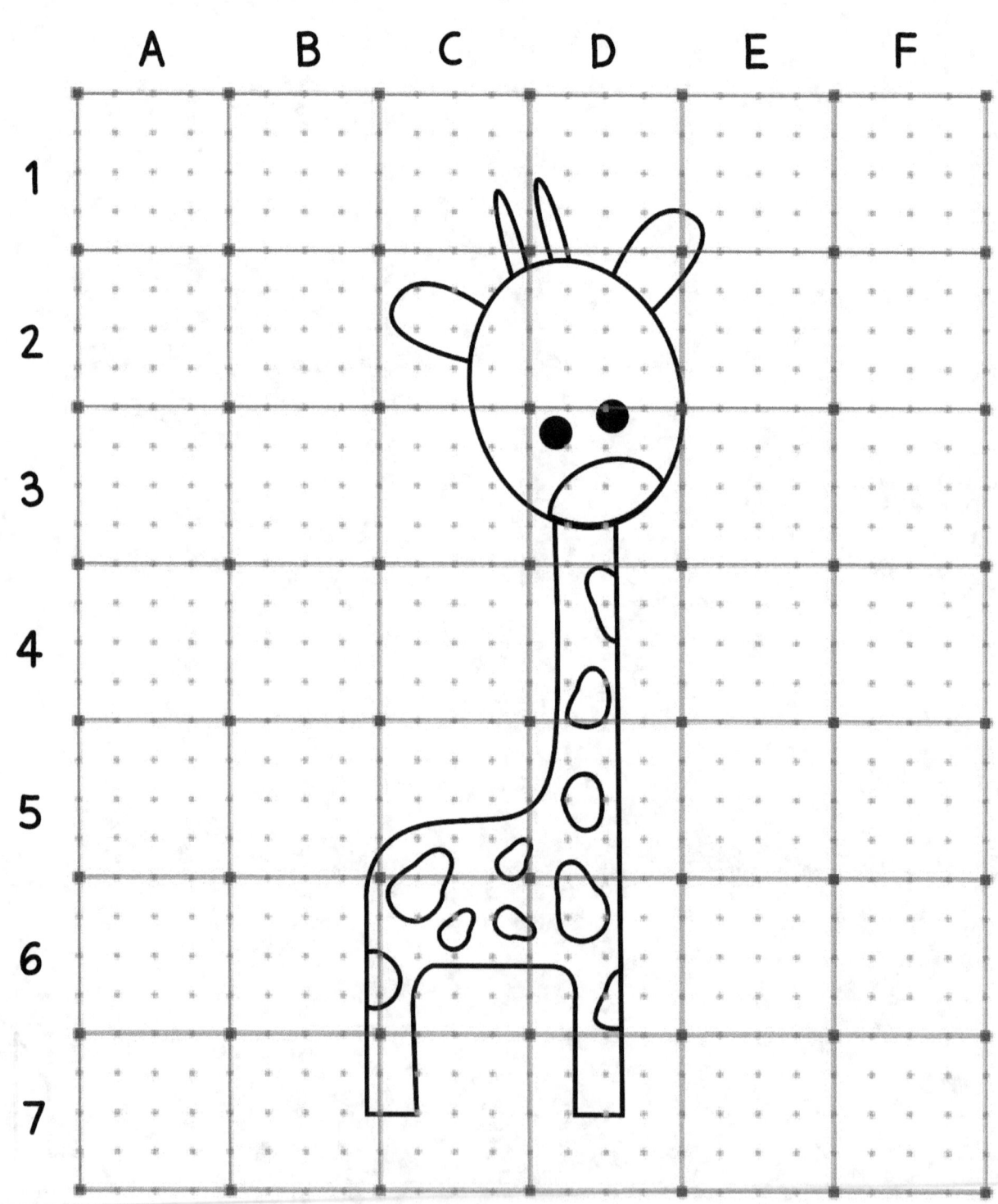

Let's Draw!

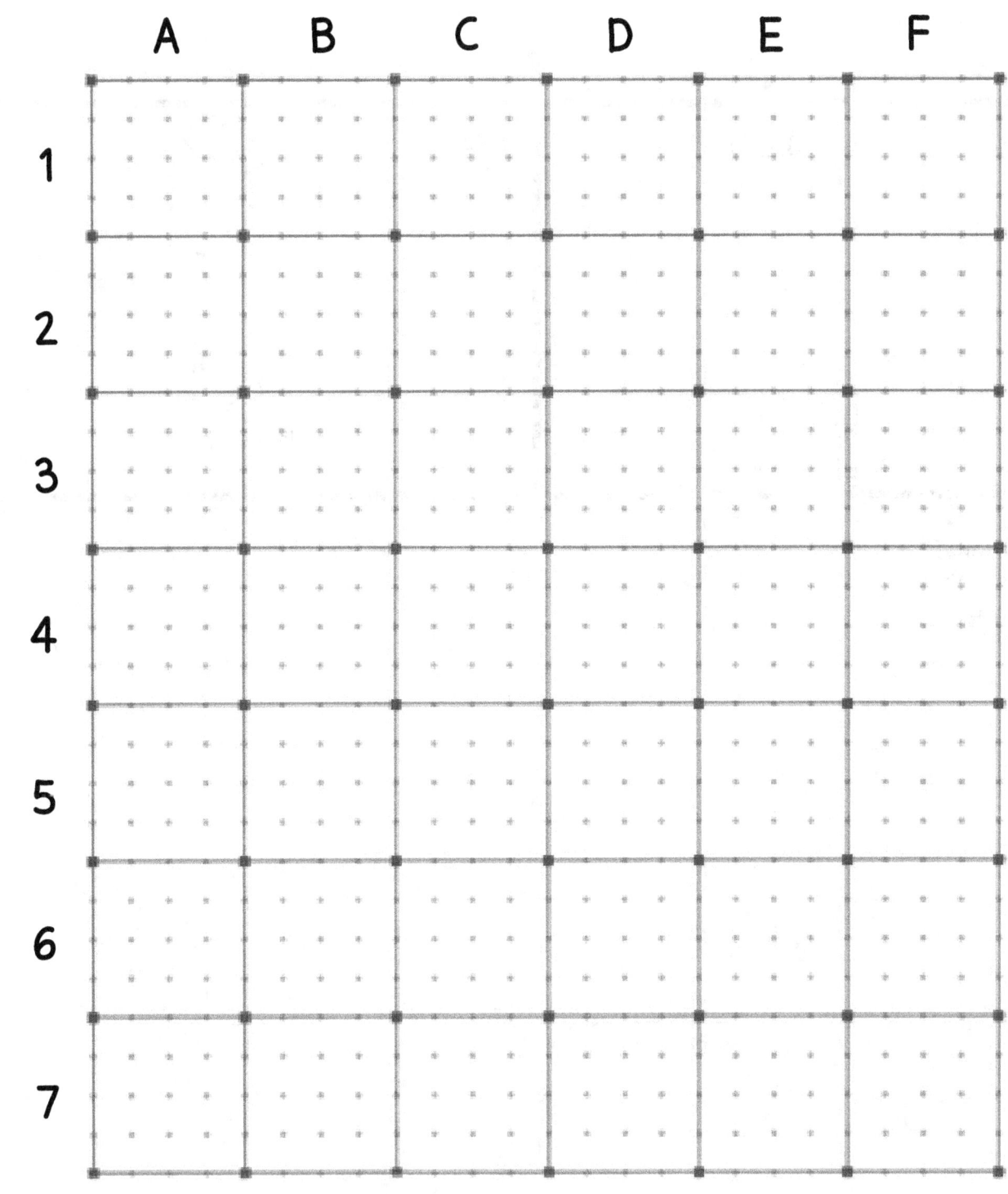

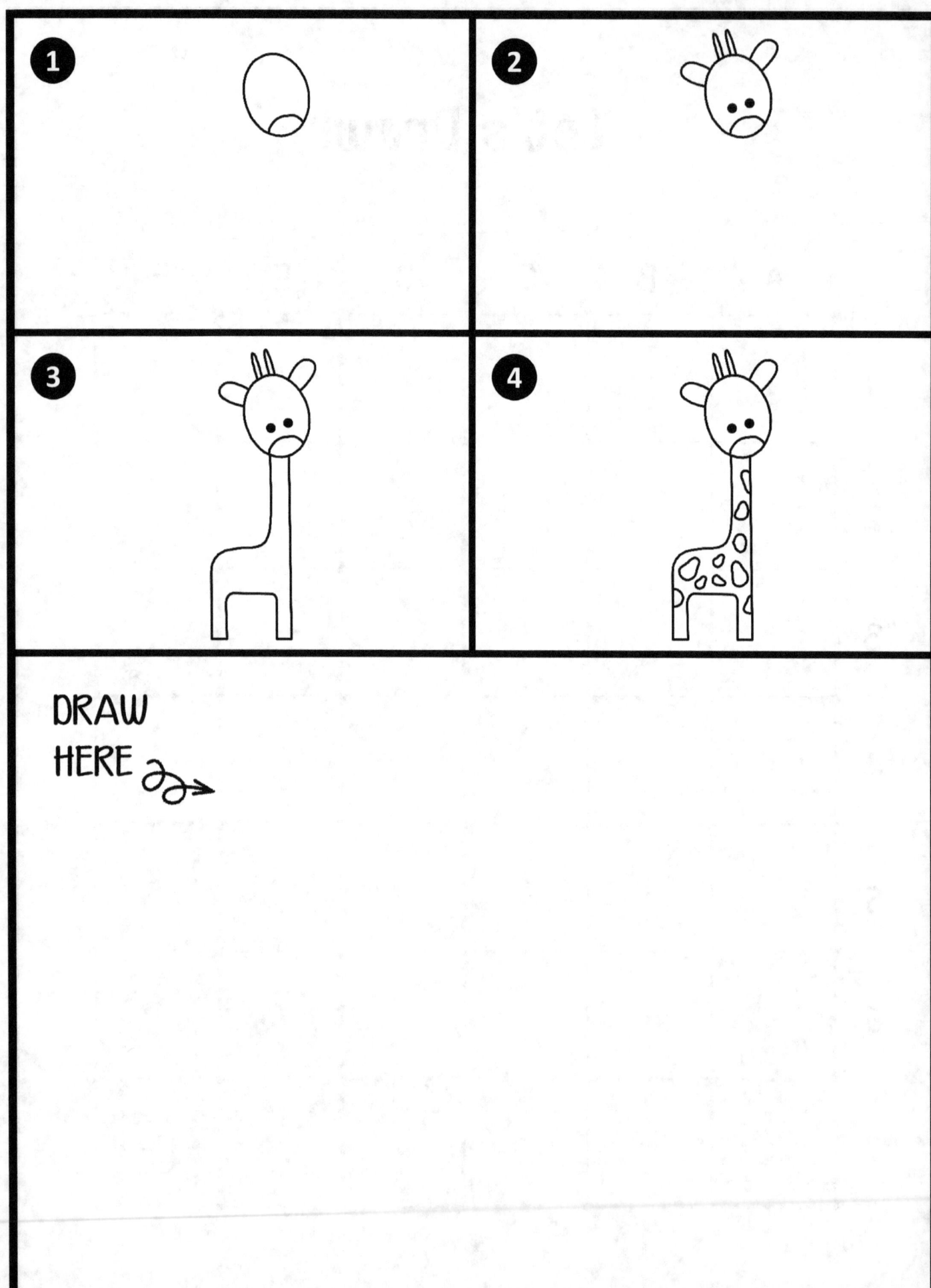

Practice

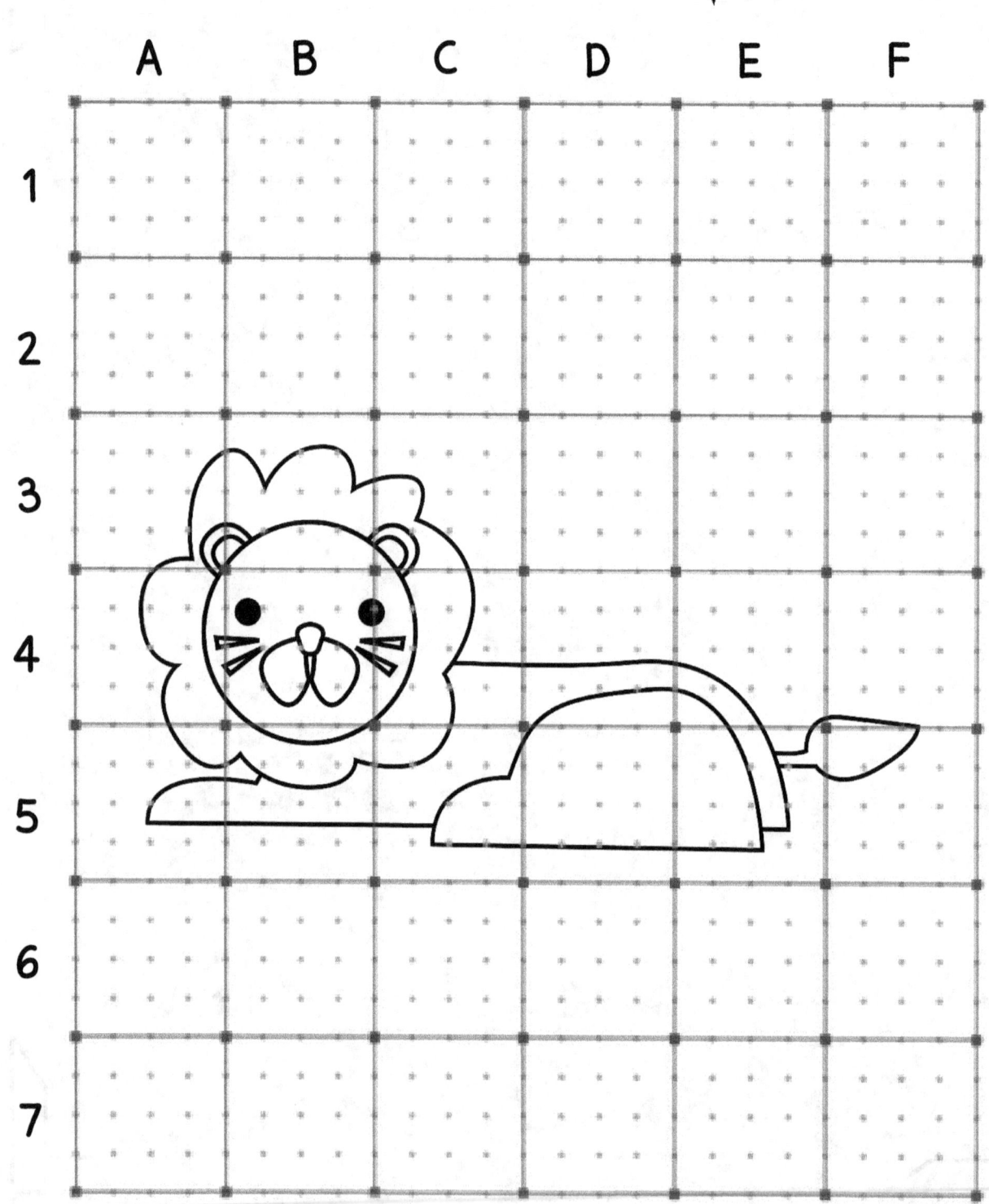

Let's Draw!

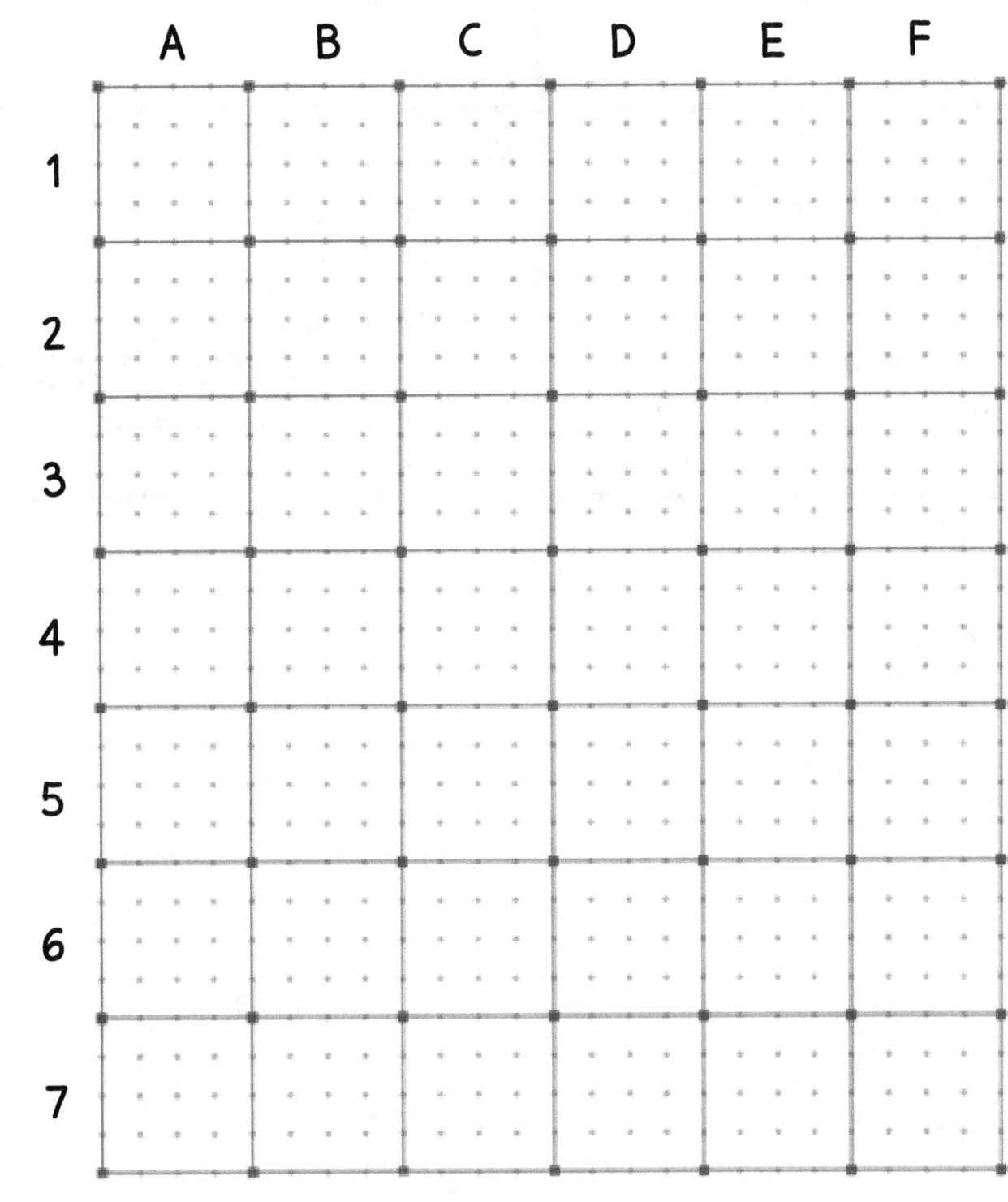

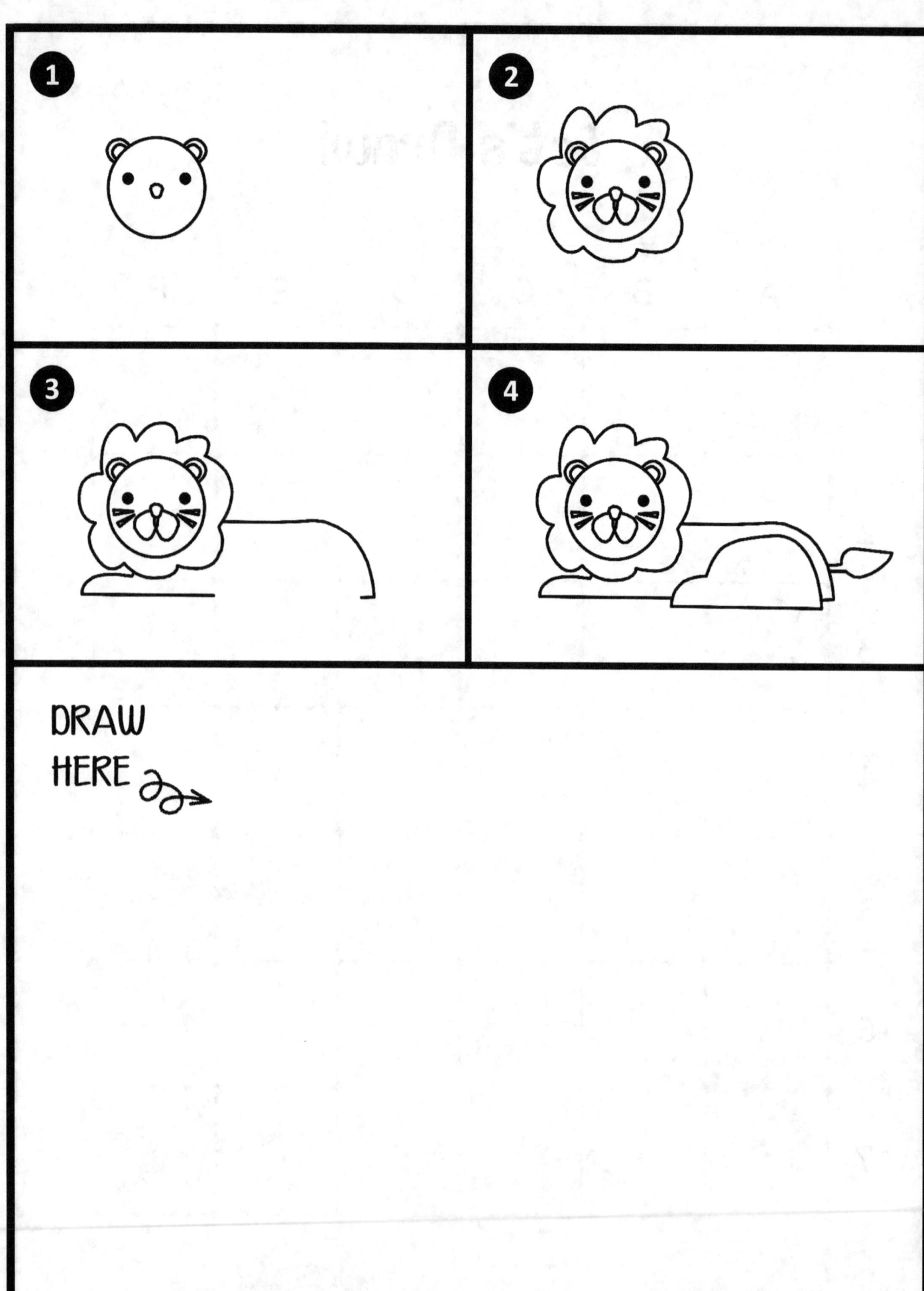

Practice

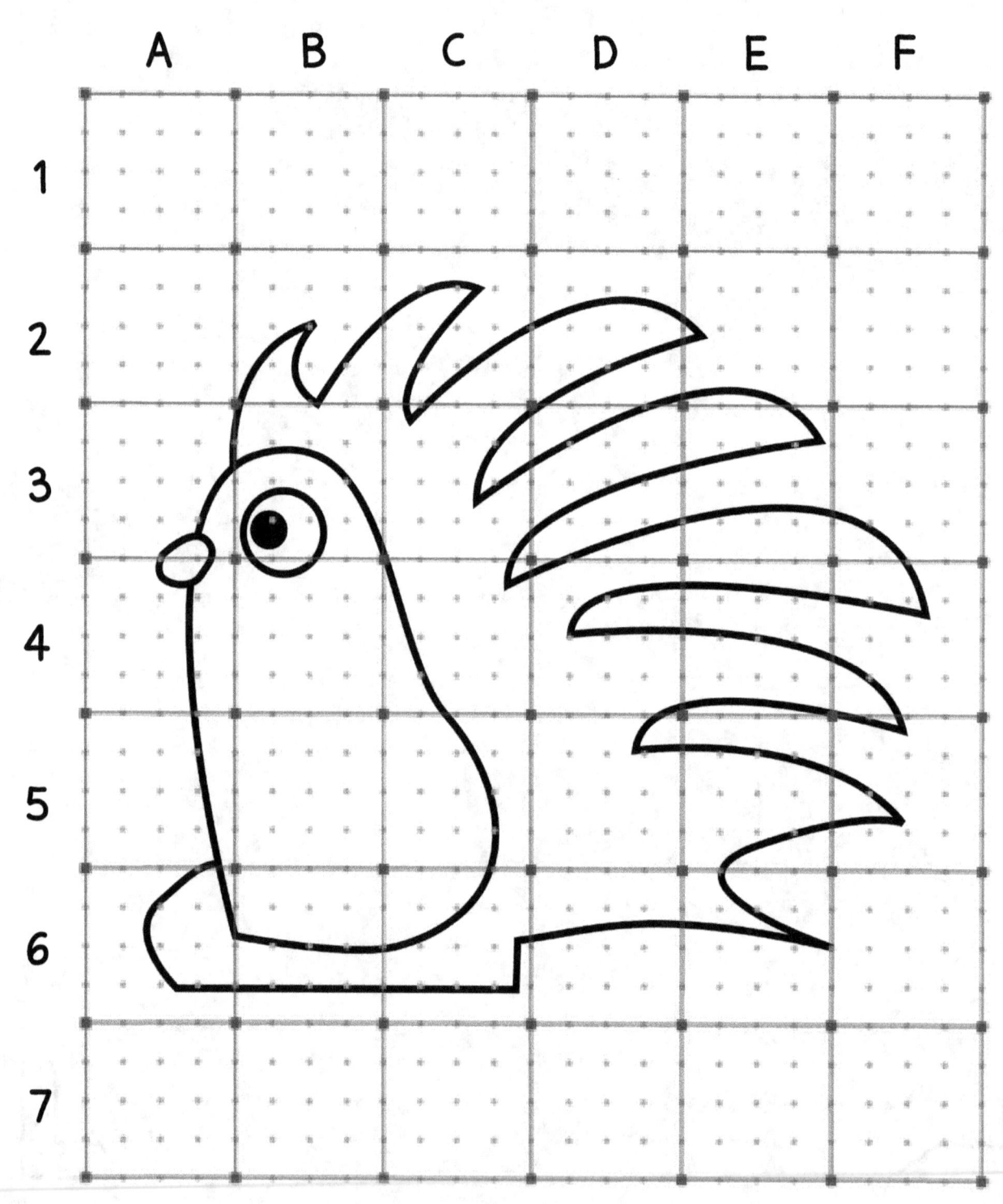

Let's Draw!

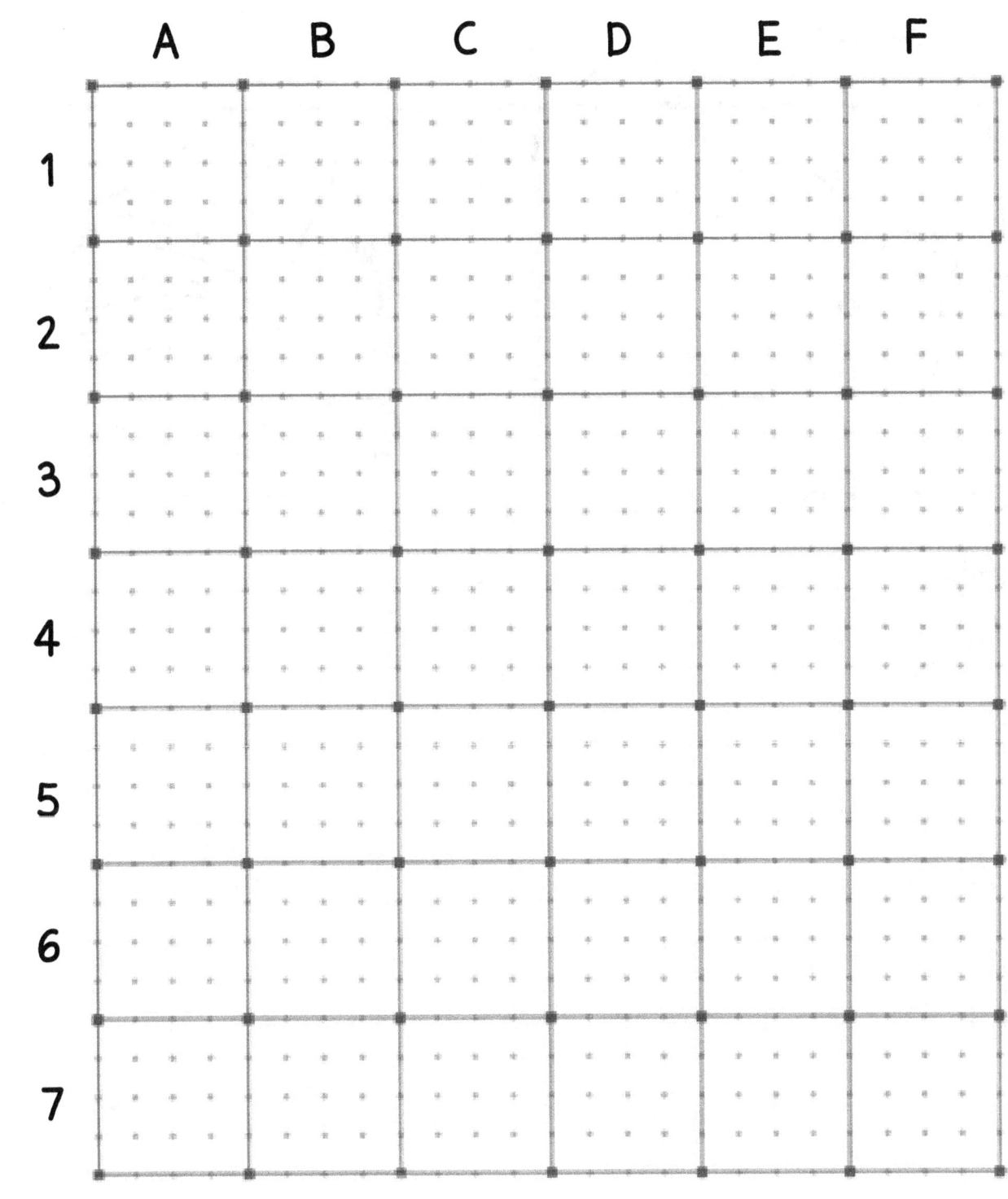

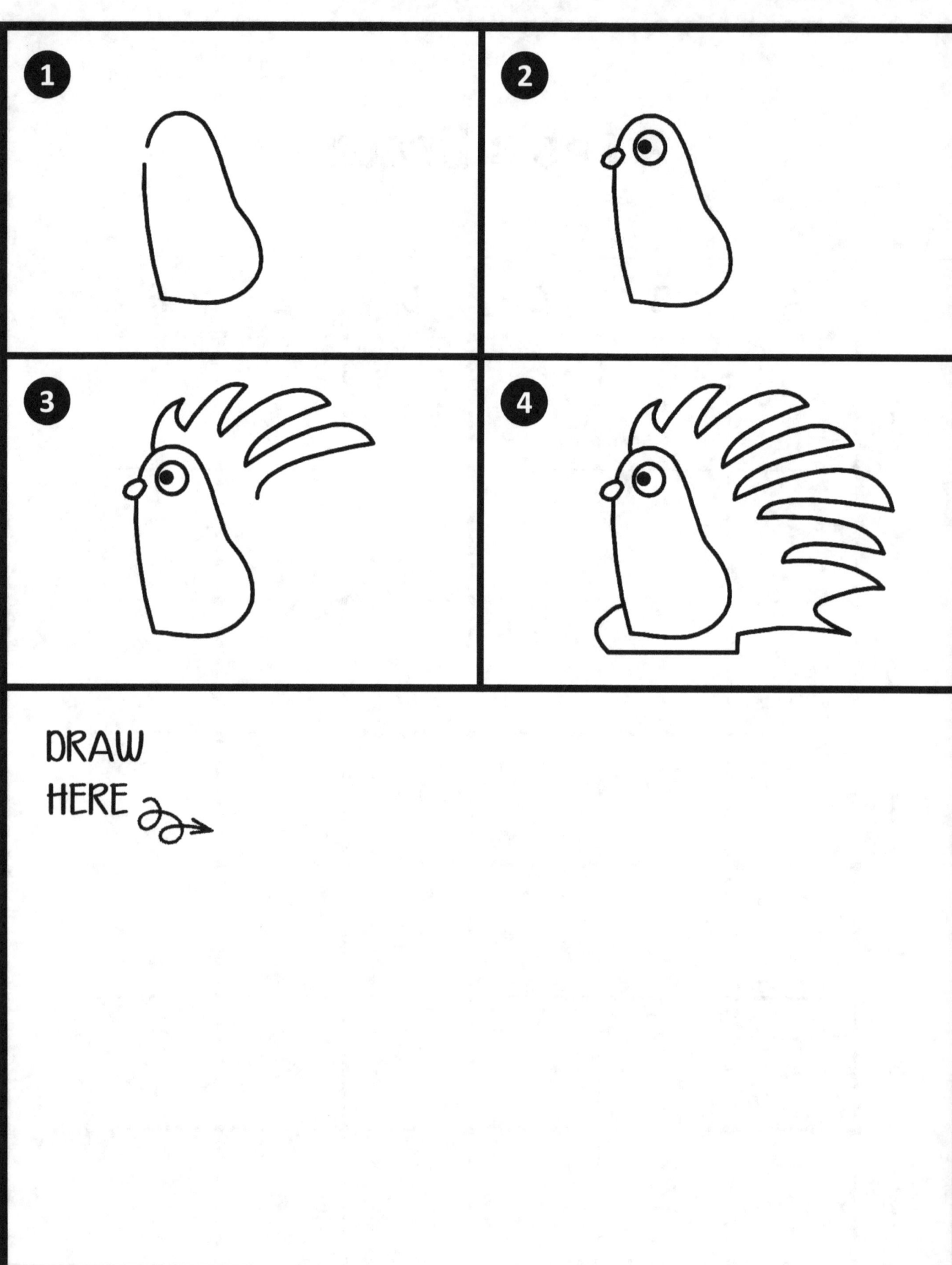

Practice

Practice

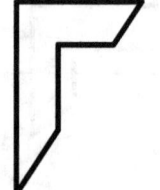
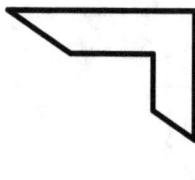
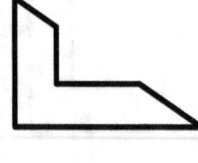
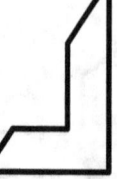

www.ingramcontent.com/pod-product-compliance
Lightning Source LLC
Chambersburg PA
CBHW060435220526
45465CB00008B/3155